WASHOE COUNTY LIBRARY

3 1235 02821 7748

5-19-03

P9-EDH-207

CHILDREN'S
LIBRARY

SP

No Longer Property of
Washoe County Library

No Longer Property of
Washoe County Library

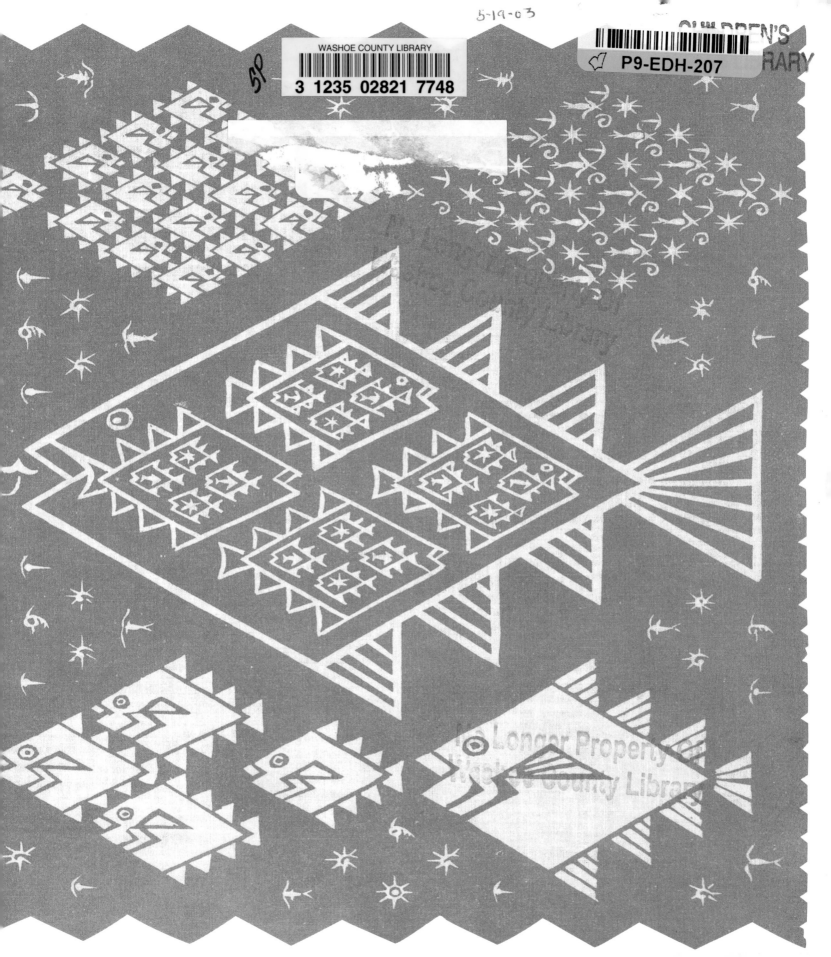

Virginia Lee Burton: A Life in Art

VIRGINIA LEE BURTON
A LIFE IN ART

by Barbara Elleman

Houghton Mifflin Company ▪ Boston 2002

Copyright © 2002 by Barbara Elleman

All rights reserved. For information about permission to reproduce selections from this book, write to
Permissions, Houghton Mifflin Company, 215 Park Avenue South, New York, New York 10003.

*While every effort has been made to obtain permission to reprint copyrighted material, there may be cases where we
have been unable to trace a copyright holder. The publisher will be happy to correct any omission in future printings.*

www.houghtonmifflinbooks.com

Book design by Lisa Diercks
The text of this book is set in Dante.
Photograph, p. ii: Courtesy of the Demetrios family
Illustration, p. v: from undated sketchbook, Cape Ann Historical Association
Photographs, pp. 2 and 4 by Andrew Brilliant/www.brilliantpictures.com
The photo on page 47 first appeared in *The Christian Science Monitor* on January 24, 1944, and is reproduced
with permission. © 1944 The Christian Science Monitor (www.csmonitor.com). All rights reserved.
Illustration, p. 65: from *Bill Peet: An Autobiography.* Copyright © 1989 by Bill Peet. Reprinted by permission
of Houghton Mifflin Company. All rights reserved.
Images running along tops of chapter openers are taken from Burton's Folly Cove designs, featured also
on pages 68, 70, 73, 74, 78, and 81.

Library of Congress Cataloging-in-Publication Data
Elleman, Barbara.
Virginia Lee Burton : a life in art / by Barbara Elleman.
      p. cm.
    Summary: Examines the life, career, artistic style, and literary themes of the twentieth-century author
and illustrator of such classic picture books as "Mike Mulligan and His Steam Shovel" and "The Little
House." Includes bibliographical references and index.
ISBN 0-618-00342-8
    1. Burton, Virginia Lee, 1909–1968—Juvenile literature. 2. Authors, American—20th century—
Biography—Juvenile literature. 3. Illustrators—United States—Biography—Juvenile literature.
4. Children's stories—Authorship—Juvenile literature. 5. Illustration of books—Juvenile literature.
[1. Burton, Virginia Lee, 1909–1968. 2. Authors, American. 3. Illustrators. 4. Authorship.
5. Illustration of books. 6. Women—Biography.] I. Title.
    PS3503.U738 Z65 2002   813'.52—dc21   2002000220

Printed in Singapore
TWP 10 9 8 7 6 5 4 3 2 1

TO ARIS AND MIKE,

WHO LIVED THE STORY

CONTENTS

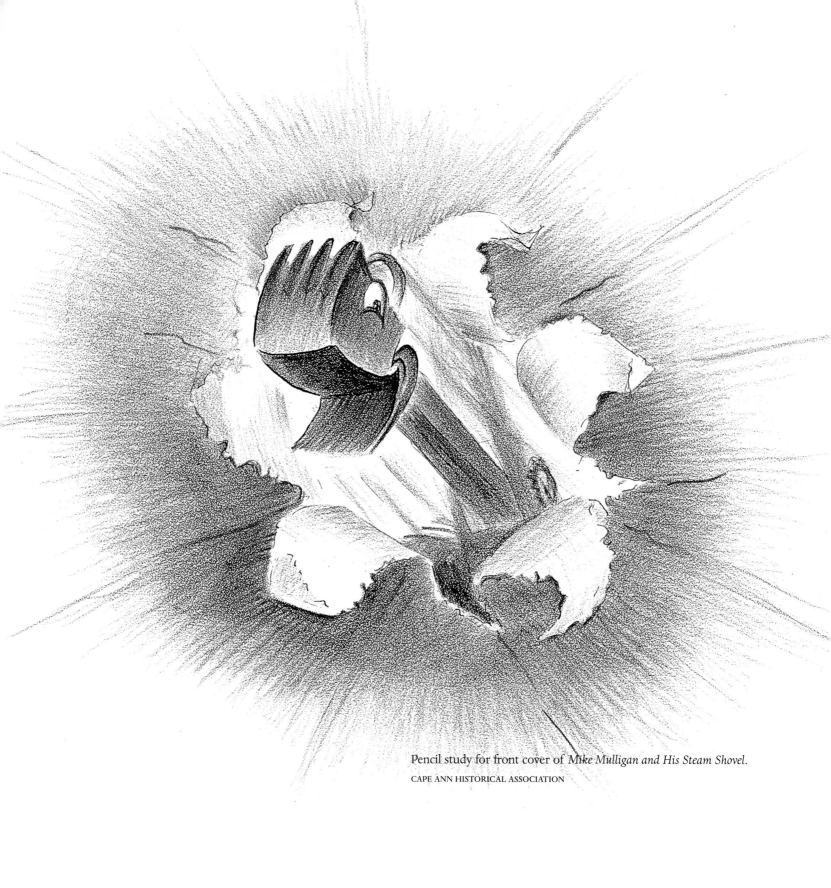

Pencil study for front cover of *Mike Mulligan and His Steam Shovel*.
CAPE ANN HISTORICAL ASSOCIATION

1 MARY ANNE TURNS SIXTY

MARY ANNE WOULD HAVE BEEN PLEASED. BACKHOES, DIGGERS, AND dump trucks, poised for work, waited expectantly to grunt and groan into action. A challenge to get moving, to get something done, seemed to permeate the air. Although she hadn't been active for sixty years, the old steam shovel's spirit clearly reverberated across the construction site on a sun-warmed November day.

The setting was West Roxbury, a Boston suburb along the banks of the Charles River, where a landfill was being turned into a new community park. The day of the groundbreaking, November 13, 1999, was the sixtieth anniversary of the publication of Virginia Lee Burton's *Mike Mulligan and His Steam Shovel* and had been proclaimed Mike Mulligan Day. Hundreds turned out for the celebration. Children, bursting with excitement and wearing bright yellow hard hats, joined Boston's mayor, Houghton Mifflin publishing personnel, journalists, and jovial bystanders to honor Mike and Mary Anne.

A group of children led participants in a hearty chorus of "Happy Birthday," and families munched on slices of enormous cakes shaped like the steam shovel, but the biggest activity focused on the dirt piles unearthed by the rigs. Children exuberantly dug holes, created walls, and

excavated foundations. Lines of youngsters formed, waiting to be lifted into the machine cabs.

On the dais that day, Burton's sons stood proudly: Aristides Burton Demetrios, whose friendly smile resembles his mother's, and Michael Burton Demetrios, whose affectionate laugh rang out over the festivities. Both residents of California, the men spoke of an idyllic childhood, of growing up in the relative isolation of Cape Ann (Massachusetts) in the 1930s and 1940s, and of their artistic parents' influence on their lives. Michael, four years old when *Mike Mulligan* was written and the model for the little boy in the book, reflected on how the story evolved. "As my mother wrote it, she read portions to me, my brother, and a handful of

Burton's sons Aris, with his wife, Ilene (*left*), and Mike, with his wife, Eleanor (*right*), are joined by Dick Berkenbush, holding a toy model of Mary Anne, in front of the steam-shovel-shaped cake.
PHOTOGRAPH BY ANDREW BRILLIANT

To the delight of children and adults alike, construction vehicles were on hand to celebrate Mike Mulligan Day in Boston, November 13, 1999.
COURTESY OF DON ELLEMAN

other neighborhood children, to test it out," he recalled. "If we started to fidget around, she'd say: 'It's back to the drawing board.' She knew she had the right text when all the kids were attentive until the end."

Another man in the crowd that day also played a role in the writing of *Mike Mulligan*. Dick Berkenbush, now in his seventies, was thirteen when Burton went to visit her longtime friend, Hazel Albertson, Berkenbush's grandmother, in West Newbury. Burton described a book she was working on: "I've got myself a problem. I dug the steam shovel into the town-hall cellar, and now I don't know how to get it out." Berkenbush pondered what he would do with a steam shovel stuck in a basement, and before dinner was over he spoke up: "Why not leave it in the cellar for a furnace?"

Two years later, Dickie, as he was then called, received an autographed copy of *Mike Mulligan* in the mail. Following an asterisk next to the line "Let her be the furnace for the new town hall," he saw, printed at the bottom of the page: "Acknowledgments to Dickie Birkenbush." Although his last name had been misspelled, "We never bothered to change it," he said laughingly. "I call it my pen name."

As the day's activities drew to a close, the Demetrios brothers, sporting hard hats and red Mike Mulligan buttons, made an announcement. Aris, a renowned sculptor whose works appear throughout the United States, would create a small bronze replica of Mary Anne to stand in the new Millennium Park. It would be a continuing tribute not only to his mother's books and to the thousands of readers who have treasured *Mike*

Under the watchful eyes of construction workers, children could become, for a moment, Mike Mulligan, turning the wheels, shifting the gears, working the pedals. PHOTOGRAPH BY ANDREW BRILLIANT

Dickie Birkenbush (with an *i*) is acknowledged in every one of the more than 1.7 million copies of *Mike Mulligan and His Steam Shovel* in print today.

MIKE MULLIGAN AND HIS STEAM SHOVEL

Now the little boy,
who had been keeping very quiet,
had another good idea.
He said,
'Why couldn't we leave Mary Anne in the cellar
and build the new town hall above her?
Let her be the furnace for the new town hall *
and let Mike Mulligan be the janitor.
Then you wouldn't have to buy a new furnace,
and we could pay Mike Mulligan
for digging the cellar
in just one day.'

* Acknowledgments to Dickie Birkenbush.

Mulligan over the years but also to the memory of those once hardworking machines.

Steam shovels, as predicted in the story, are no longer a part of the construction scene, but children still love Mike and Mary Anne. "There seems little difference in these kids than when we were young," Aris commented, "roughhousing, playing with dirt, fascinated by machines. Perhaps it's not such a long time ago, after all."

Family portrait in the backyard in Folly Cove, circa 1942. *From left:* nephew Costa Maletskos, son Aris, Virginia Lee Burton, son Mike, and husband George Demetrios.

COURTESY OF COSTA MALETSKOS

2 FAMILY ROOTS

VIRGINIA LEE BURTON WAS BORN ON AUGUST 30, 1909, IN NEWTON Center, Massachusetts, to Lena Dalkeith Yates and Alfred Edgar Burton. The combined aesthetic genes of these two highly individualistic, iconoclastic people would have an impact on all of their three children, and particularly on their daughter Virginia.

Alfred Burton, born in Portland, Maine, in 1857, graduated from nearby Bowdoin College in 1878 with a degree in engineering. His zest for adventure led him to join several scientific expeditions, including one in 1896 to Greenland with the renowned Admiral Robert Perry (also a Bowdoin graduate). About the same time Alfred made a trip to Rotterdam, where he gained valuable firsthand knowledge of water control, which he later applied to Boston's Charles River basin. Eventually he was instrumental in determining the site for the present Massachusetts Institute of Technology. Highly regarded for his intellect and leadership, Alfred was named the first dean of MIT, in 1902. Citations about his accomplishments often refer to him as the "beloved" dean.

An early marriage to Gertrude Hitz in 1884 ended with her death. The younger of their two children, Felix Arnold Burton, an architect, designed several buildings for Bowdoin, from which he also graduated. The older,

Harold Burton, enjoyed a distinguished career as the mayor of Cleveland, Ohio; a senator; and a Supreme Court justice. Appointed by President Truman, Harold Burton served the Court from 1945 to 1958. Although autobiographical materials written by Virginia Burton do not mention her two half-brothers, a letter from Harold, written on U.S. Supreme Court stationery, congratulates her on the publication of *Life Story* and suggests a warm relationship between them. Both men, according to Virginia's sons, were always a part of the large extended family that gathered around their parents.

Virginia Burton's mother, Lena Yates, was English. Although there has been some disagreement about where and when she was born — an article in *Western American Literature* states she was born in Stockport, Cheshire, in 1879, while a Carl Cherry Foundation brochure lists her birth as 1887 in Donnisthorpe, England — it is now generally agreed that 1879 is closer to the correct date. Lena's father, a seed merchant, deserted the family early, and Lena and her mother moved to Scotland and later to London and Paris. An eccentric woman, Lena took various names over her lifetime. She wrote several books as Lena Dalkeith, a name she reportedly borrowed from a village near Edinburgh, and she also used the pseudonym Juniper Green and later became Jeanne D'Orge. Writing was part of her life from an early age; by the time she was twenty, she had published a number of children's books, including *Aesop's Fables, Little Plays,* and *Stories from French History*.

On a walking trip in France in 1906, she met Alfred Burton, many years her senior, and married him not long after. Lena returned with him to Newton Center, Massachusetts, where she continued her writing pursuits. In 1913, Lena was invited to read her poetry, described as surrealistic

These and the following photographs of Virginia as a young woman reflect her vibrancy and spontaneity. COURTESY OF THE DEMETRIOS FAMILY

"feverish prose poems," at the New York Armory Show, and in 1915 she published a collection of verse, *Prose Chants* (the only known publication bearing the name Lena Dalkeith Burton).

Within a few years three children were born: Christine, Virginia, and Alexander Ross. Though only a few details are known of Virginia's childhood years, a feeling of family unity and happiness and certainly of her artistic roots comes through in an autobiographical piece she wrote for Houghton Mifflin: "My memories of early childhood in Newton Center consist of English folk songs and English folk dancing around a Maypole [and] celebrating Twelfth Night when everyone dressed up in costumes and the neighbors came in to sing and dance and 'wassail' the old apple trees. On other holidays our parents put on marionette shows for us and our friends. Our old barn was converted into a school and I believe the first Montessori System in this country was taught there." She instilled this sense of play and love for dance and music in her own children when they were growing up. She also tells of her early exposure to books: "Dad, instead of giving us toys for birthdays and Christmas gave us beautifully illustrated children's books which he would read aloud to us. I am sure my interest in picture books stemmed from this." One of her favorite tales was Hans Christian Andersen's "The Emperor's New Clothes," which she later adapted and illustrated.

But unsettling events disturbed this idyllic time. Citing poor health (what may have been tuberculosis), Lena relocated the children to California, first to San Diego and then, in 1920, at the suggestion of her friend, the painter Marsden Hartley, to Carmel-by-the-Sea. At the time, this center of artistic bohemians included such luminaries as John Steinbeck, Lincoln Steffens, Robinson Jeffers, and Ansel Adams, which greatly appealed

to the outgoing, creative Lena. The West Coast ambience evidently agreed with her, and she lived into her mid-eighties.

Although these moves were no doubt disconcerting, Virginia warmly describes the change of scene: "Carmel was then a simple unspoiled small town inhabited by retired and semi-retired artists, writers, and musicians. There were three theaters and a little old two-room schoolhouse. Always there was a play or an operetta in rehearsal going on and everybody took part. To be sure it was all amateur, but it was a lot of fun. My sister and I loved dancing and studied at every opportunity (of which there were many) and appeared in the local productions."

Alfred Burton joined Lena and the children in Carmel after his retirement from MIT in 1921, but the marriage didn't last. A former MIT student, Carl Cherry, arrived on the scene, and three years later Lena Burton left her husband and children to live with this man twenty-four years her junior (about the same age difference as between her and her older husband). Carl, an inventor with a special interest in mechanical toys and offbeat gadgets, was considered by some to be a crank and highly impractical. He and Lena eventually married, and although they lived in poverty for many years, his invention of the Cherry rivet, which revolutionized the manufacture of aircraft in World War II, made him a millionaire. The patent was eventually purchased by the Textron Company, which still produces the Cherry rivet today. Unfortunately, Carl didn't live long enough to enjoy the rewards; he died in 1947.

Lena began using the name Jeanne D'Orge full-time when she went to live with Carl Cherry. The moniker was supposedly a combined nod to her heroine Joan of Arc and the Orge River in France. Her reputation in Carmel as a talented poet, playwright, and mystic later expanded to

Expectations of a dance career sent Virginia east in 1928, around the time this photo was taken. COURTESY OF THE DEMETRIOS FAMILY

include the role of artist when she took up painting. Some of her works resembled Chinese landscapes; others were more surreal and abstract.

Following Carl's death, Jeanne established the Carl Cherry Foundation, a nonprofit art center, in Carmel. Jeanne's papers, a permanent art collection of twelve hundred works from her portfolio, and some memorabilia are there, as is a miscellaneous assortment of Burton family artifacts. Although Virginia inherited her mother's artistic tendencies, their work shows little resemblance. The precision, fine detail, rhythmic design, and overarching spirit of Virginia Lee Burton's illustrations bear few similarities to her mother's paintings.

By the time Jeanne died in 1964, she was known as a warm, compassionate woman, and she was eulogized as an "ancient and honorable citizen of Carmel." However, her desertion of her husband and children in 1925 scandalized the community. According to Virginia's son Michael,

Burton's mother, Jeanne D'Orge, painted abstract images that were often executed in dark, broad strokes. COURTESY OF CARL CHERRY CENTER FOR THE ARTS

Jeanne woke her children in the middle of the night and told them that she was moving down the street to live with Carl Cherry.

While her mother's actions must have had a devastating effect on Virginia, then sixteen, her sons maintain that it didn't affect her overall positive outlook. Instead, Aris says, "my mother had a natural affinity for life; bitterness had no role." She created a "wonderful world" for her children to grow up in, he says. "I think she was determined not to visit on her children what happened to her: a mother that abandoned her husband and family, children that were separated and uprooted." Virginia was sent to live with a family in Sonora, California. Although in later years Virginia reconciled with her mother, traveling regularly to California to visit her, Christine and Alexander reportedly had little or no contact with Jeanne for the rest of their lives.

Virginia performing "The Laughing Dance" in a recital in the mid-1920s.
COURTESY OF THE DEMETRIOS FAMILY

Perhaps as a buffer to the turbulence in her adolescent years, Virginia turned her energies to the arts. In her junior year, she won a scholarship to the California School of Fine Arts, where studies provided a basis for the artistic career that was to come. Even in high school, her leadership abilities and creativity were evident. At Sonora High School, she served as editor of the Green and Gold, the high school yearbook, and participated in various theatricals. Prior to her graduation in 1927, Virginia successfully staged a dance recital at the school in which a dozen-plus students performed a minuet, a Hungarian dance, a Cossack ensemble, and other numbers. After high school, Burton remarked, "Having no

Found in one of Burton's (undated) sketchbooks, these line drawings display her early ability to portray subtle nuances of the human figure.
CAPE ANN HISTORICAL ASSOCIATION

desire to go to college, I thought I might as well go to art school and continue studying dancing with a good ballet teacher in San Francisco, which I did." She studied dance under Muriel Stuart, a student of the famed Anna Pavlova, and art and design with Robert Hestwood, a printmaker and teacher, and his wife. To attend classes she needed to travel by rail, ferry boat, and cable car: "I used those long commuting hours to train myself in making quick sketches from life and from memory of my unaware fellow passengers."

Meanwhile, her older sister, Christine, who was now an accomplished dancer and would later establish a dance studio in Plainfield, New Jersey, had accepted a contract with a vaudeville dance group in New York City. Virginia's father had returned to Boston, following his marriage breakup, and in 1928, Virginia went east also. "There was a chance for me to join her troupe," she related, "and I had even signed the contract when my father broke his leg. I stayed home to take care of him and that was the beginning and end of my dancing career, which was just as well, because I wasn't very good, anyway."

In one respect, Alfred Burton's broken leg was fortuitous: it channeled Burton's career away from dance and into illustration. While keeping house for her father, Burton occupied herself with a number of different jobs. She taught art at the Burroughs Newsboys Foundation and worked as a lifeguard, swimming instructor, and art counselor at a YMCA summer camp. But her most influential job, certainly, was as illustrator for the *Boston Transcript* newspaper in the late 1920s and early 1930s. Virginia's job involved accompanying a well-known drama and music critic of the time, known only as H.T.P., to plays and musical events, to create visual profiles for the paper, which she usually signed VLeeB. In particularly enlightening images she depicted Katherine Cornell as Countess Olenska and Katherine Stewart as Mrs. Mingott in the Boston opening of a theatrical adaptation of Edith Wharton's *Age of Innocence*. Virginia, only twenty at the time, produced skillfully caricatured sketches full of life, energy, and wit. If the images she drew for her own amusement on the ferry boats and cable cars in San Francisco were practice sessions, then this experience provided vigorous workouts for the finely honed portrayals that would eventually personalize her books.

Virginia's life was to take a pivotal turn in the fall of 1930. "Through mutual friends," she wrote, "I had heard of George Demetrios and what a great teacher of sculpture and drawing he was, so in the fall of 1930 when I was twenty-one, I enrolled in his Saturday morning drawing class

Facing page: Burton sketched many theatrical, musical, and sports personalities in her work for the *Boston Transcript;* here, she drew Broadway star Katherine Cornell in her role as Countess Olenska. Burton was praised for her "gift of capturing fleeting action" in an extensive exhibition of these drawings at the Boston Public Library. BOSTON TRANSCRIPT, OCTOBER 26, 1929. MICROFILM PRINT COURTESY OF BOSTON PUBLIC LIBRARY

at the Boston Museum School." An immediate attraction and rapport occurred between the tall, solidly built, raven-haired George and the petite, brown-haired Virginia, whom a friend called a "classic New England beauty." Less than a year later, on March 28, 1931, they were married.

In 1911, George, a Greek immigrant, had arrived in the United States at age fifteen with a nametag attached to his lapel. Although he spoke no English, Greek music in the streets of Boston led him to a community of fellow countrymen. There, an extraordinary thing happened. To earn money, George shined shoes on the street. During slow times, he amused himself by drawing faces of the people he saw. One day a man, illustrator and painter John Hybers, saw George's sketches and, very impressed, arranged for him to receive a scholarship, funded by art enthusiast Charlotte Hallowell of West Medford, to the School of the Museum of Fine Arts in Boston. George quickly became a star pupil of the highly regarded artist and teacher Charles Grafly and was declared a genius by those who saw his work. In less than five years after arriving in the United States, Demetrios was awarded the coveted Edmund Stewardson Prize for figure modeling by the Pennsylvania Academy of the Fine Arts. In the early 1920s, he went to France to study at the École des Beaux Arts and at the Sorbonne, where he developed a "brilliant fluency" of line. A visit to the prehistoric caves in southern France made an indelible impression: The cave paintings,

George Demetrios, by J.A.H. (probably John Hybers), 1913. COURTESY OF THE DEMETRIOS FAMILY

obviously drawn from events in action, convinced him that drawing from life was the best way to capture the realism he wanted to portray in his work.

Back in America, George directed his interest to teaching life drawing classes and creating sculptural works at the Boston Museum School. His reputation grew, and soon his work was featured in several highly esteemed exhibitions. In 1927, he opened the George Demetrios School of Drawing and Sculpture in Boston. Summer classes were held in Charles Grafly's old studio in Folly Cove, on the north shore of Massachusetts, which George had inherited following his mentor's death. Throughout his lifetime, George was highly regarded as a teacher, sculptor, draftsman, and linguist; in addition, he wrote two well-received books, *When I Was a Boy in Greece* and *When Greek Meets Greek*.

Following their marriage, Virginia and George lived for a year in Lincoln, Massachusetts, where their first son, Aristides Burton Demetrios, was born on February 17, 1932. Then, drawn to the rural coastal setting of Cape Ann, which George had first come to love when visiting Grafly, they moved to Folly Cove in Gloucester. After renting for a year, the couple bought a small, turn-of-the-century house that became the anchor of their gregarious lifestyle. Set near the coast, it provided the quiet oasis they desired; they lived there the rest of their lives. Michael, their second child, was born there on August 30, 1936, his mother's birthday. This dual celebration motivated many exuberant daylong parties full of baseball, dancing, games, and hearty home-cooked meals.

A nephew, Costa Maletskos, who spent many summers with the Demetrioses, remarked, "There was a distinct aura that these two artists created as they went about their lives. It profoundly influenced their own way of living and that of their sons, and it brought forth an ambience that overflowed to the many friends and family who gravitated to their home over the years." The strength they drew—individually and together—from the natural beauty of the area and their mutual belief in

Virginia, Mike, and Aris in the late 1930s. COURTESY OF THE DEMETRIOS FAMILY

the inherent artistic ability of all individuals inspired the enthusiasm and devotion of countless pupils.

In a 1963 Gloucester newspaper article, reporter Virginia Bohlin described their home: "The house is surrounded by seven and a half acres which George has landscaped with flowers, a babbling brook, a natural pool, and stepping stone paths. Here and there are spotted some of Demetrios's sculpture — 'The Sauna' encircled in a bed of red and white petunias on the hillside; 'The Sun Bather' relaxing in the middle of the fern-bordered pool in the woods." The house, which originally sat close to noisy Route 127, was moved back onto a gentle knoll in an apple orchard. Some ten years later, this move inspired Burton's Caldecott Medal–winning book, *The Little House*. The property included her studio, near the house, and his — a large barnlike structure he built among the trees where he worked on his own creations.

Bohlin paints the picture further: "Out front graze their Cheviot sheep. And between the sheep pasture and the house is George's vegetable garden where he grows eggplants, tomatoes, corn, carrots, all kinds of lettuce and greens, beets, leeks, Italian parsley, [and] peppers. . . . George does the gardening in the late afternoon after his sculpturing classes and about the time Virginia, or Jinnee as he calls his wife, heads from her studio to their big country kitchen to prepare dinner. Jinnee loves to cook and it's usually a gourmet meal, with maybe a first course of the delectable fish chowder she makes." Meals, her sons remember, were a special time, served in the summer on a polished granite picnic table, which

Mike and his mother pose next to their birthday cake, made by cousin Costa Maletskos and uncle Constantine Pappis. There was a pond of blue gelatin next to the edible house, a miniature of their Folly Cove home.
COURTESY OF COSTA MALETSKOS

today still stands between the house and Virginia's studio. The table, four and a half tons' worth, was made from local granite intended for a New York bank but rejected because of a dark spot. Virginia thought it "a perfect table; you never need a cloth, and when you want to wash the table, all you have to do is turn a hose on it."

Music was ever present. A record player, with a speaker on wheels so that it could be brought to the barn window, sometimes played classical, sometimes folk music. Virginia had an enormous record collection, and melodies of all kinds floated across the lawn, depending on the occasion. Connecting all this was Virginia's charisma, creating a harmony between work and leisure. One gets the impression that a special

Bottle-feeding their Cheviot lambs was just another task in George and Virginia's busy, creative life.
COURTESY OF LEE KINGMAN NATTI

excitement existed wherever she was—an effervescence that enlivened all she touched.

The *joie de vivre* that friends and family remember is hard, they say, to capture in words. Virginia's friend and onetime editor Lee Kingman Natti recalls: "There were marvelous parties, largely because of George's ebullient personality as host and cook. He usually roasted a sheep over an open fire. Then there was the crisp tenderness of salad greens fresh from his incredible garden. There was Jinnee's insistence that everyone dance, and George's fondness for songs in many languages. But mostly, it was Jinnee's vivaciousness and encompassing warmth that made the place so unique." Whether it was square dancing, the Finn hop, or the Viennese waltz, the floors reverberated with merriment, the echoes of which still seem to vibrate out of the old studio. Nephew Costa's wife, Mary Maletskos, relates, "When you entered Jinnee and George's driveway at Folly Cove, you might find a baseball game in the meadow, a birthday party under the apple tree, a Saturday night baked-bean or spaghetti supper, Greek dancing on the lawn, or square dancing in Jinnee's studio. I was one of the lucky ones who crossed over the threshold into the special world of Jinnee and George."

Virginia's life, already full with painting, gardening, cooking, sewing, dancing, friends, and children, was to brim with a new kind of luster when she decided to broaden her artistic skills by writing and illustrating a book for children.

Facing page: With the rise of her children's book career, Virginia, here wearing a dress made from Folly Cove fabric, relaxed by dancing, sometimes on the marble slab that served as an outdoor table. COURTESY OF COSTA MALETSKOS, 1955

An Easterly Breeze

Just for a tease

Knocked Jonnifer out

Of his dignified ease

Higgledy...piggledy

Minus his dignity

Jonnifer tumbled

In spirals and curls

Although *Jonnifer Lint* never found a publisher, the main character displays the sprightly action and sense of movement that became known as the Burton style.

UNPUBLISHED COPY OF *JONNIFER LINT*, COURTESY OF THE DEMETRIOS FAMILY

3 FROM JONNIFER TO MIKE

BURTON'S EARLY ATTEMPT TO WRITE A CHILDREN'S STORY, SHE SAID, was disastrous. "My first book, *Jonnifer Lint,* was about a piece of dust. I and my friends thought it was very clever, but thirteen publishers disagreed with us, and when I finally got the manuscript back and started to read it to Aris, age three and one half, he went to sleep before I could even finish it. That taught me a lesson, and from then on I worked with and for my audience, my own children. I would tell them the story over and over, watching their reaction and adjusting to their interest or lack of interest [and] the same with the drawings."

This early manuscript, however, must have caught the eye of an editor at Houghton Mifflin (possibly Lovell Thompson, who was head of the trade book department at that time), because Burton was asked to provide the artwork for *Sad-Faced Boy.* The 119-page novel, written by the well-regarded African American author Arna Bontemps, tells the story of three Alabama boys who ride the freight trains north in the 1930s to find out what life is like in Harlem. Burton's contribution included a story-setting frontispiece and seven full-page illustrations, some done in black and white, some brushed with shades of red and tan.

Although *Choo Choo: The Story of a Little Engine Who Ran Away* is generally regarded as Burton's first book — and it *was* the first she both wrote and illustrated — a 1939 *Horn Book* article tells a different story: "*Sad-Faced Boy* was a rush order. I had only a week to do it in and that week was a week before Christmas, which is always a busy time with me. [It] was my first illustration job. But those weren't my only problems. We live in Gloucester and much to my surprise and consternation I found that there are no negroes [*sic*] in Gloucester or on the Cape in winter. Or if there are, they are very hard to find. I called up all the schools, but there were no negro boys enrolled. So what to do for a model. There wasn't time to go to Boston and look for just the right one.

"Then I remembered an incident that happened some years ago. It was at the time of that tremendous snowstorm. My husband and I were driving from West Medford into Boston, or rather we were trying to do so, when we got held up by snowdrifts and traffic. It was in the negro section just outside Cambridge. There was nothing to do but wait till every one got shoveled out. While waiting, I happened to glance at a window looking into the street. There was a boy, a negro boy, in a bright red sweater, and beside him his little brother with his nose flattened against the window pane. But it was the older boy's face and expression that arrested my attention. He had the saddest and most wistful face I had ever seen, a face hauntingly beautiful and with the wisdom of the ages in it. A face one couldn't forget, and I didn't. As soon as we reached the studio I made a drawing of him and later a painting. I am very glad I did, because he is the boy I used for Slumber in *Sad-Faced Boy*."

Discovered in Burton's studio twenty-five years after her death, this drawing served as her model for illustrations of Slumber in *Sad-Faced Boy*. COURTESY OF THE DEMETRIOS FAMILY

SLUMBER WAS POUNDING THE BIG OLD DRUM

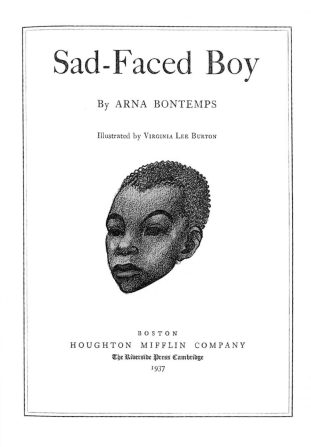

Sad-Faced Boy

By ARNA BONTEMPS

Illustrated by VIRGINIA LEE BURTON

BOSTON
HOUGHTON MIFFLIN COMPANY
The Riverside Press Cambridge
1937

Left: Slumber, a rural boy from Alabama, proudly marches down the streets of Harlem. *Right:* Burton drew her rendering of Slumber from the "hauntingly beautiful" image she had once sketched, its sculpted look undoubtedly inspired by the busts that her husband carved. SAD-FACED BOY BY ARNA BONTEMPS

This ability to capture the poignancy and expression of a real person undoubtedly stemmed from her work on the *Boston Transcript* and from her continuing studies with her husband. Her sons recall that she often found time to run up to the big studio where Dorgie, as they called their father, held classes, to refresh her eye and hand through his perceptive criticism.

Shortly after publication of *Sad-Faced Boy, Horn Book* reviewer Ione Morrison Rider credited Burton with expanding Bontemps's droll and mischievous situations. However, compared to Burton's later work, many of the pictures have a staid quality, marking a less skilled effort.

Choo Choo, which came out later that same year, 1937, was written for Burton's five-year-old son, Aris. The genesis for the book, the author said, "came from watching the engines at Rockport Station. An engine on the Gloucester branch of the Boston and Maine is the heroine. Almost every day we had to go down and see the trains come in and go out and the engines switching the coaches and freight cars around." Burton's resolve — "to try my stories on the boys first. If they like them, I feel sure other children will" — paid off. The story proved popular with children then, and it has stayed continually in print for more than sixty-five years.

Burton's illustration work actually began before her entry into children's book publishing. A songbook dated 1934 entitled *Fairies and Friendly Folk: Folk Song Pieces for the Piano,* collected by Mary Bacon Mason, lists Virginia Demetrios as the illustrator and features her supple line drawings on nearly every page.

Five years after the publication of *Choo Choo,* L. Felix Ranlett, librarian at the Bangor (Maine) Public Library, a father of three, and a writer himself, praised *Choo Choo* in the *Horn Book* for its "gusto." He defined this attribute as "[the] vigor of line and movement . . . [a] twinkle in the storyteller's eye infused into his printed words . . . [the] quick push of the artist's pencil, dashing strokes caught on paper." This "gusto" that Ranlett and his sons so enjoyed could also, he said, be found "in Robert McCloskey's *Lentil,* Ludwig Bemelmans's *Madeline,* Hardie Gramatky's *Little Toot,* and James Daugherty's *Andy and the Lion."* His words, which nimbly captured Burton's intent and style, must have been satisfying to the artist at this early stage of her career.

Decades later, in his book *Ways of the Illustrator,* Joseph Schwartz also found much to admire. He labeled the scene in which Choo Choo runs out of steam "as expressive acoustically as it is visually. Changing letter sizes, fragmented words, and dotted lines — CHOO choo ch . . . ch . . .

Facing page: From *Fairies and Friendly Folk,* the only book to carry her married name, Virginia Demetrios, which appears on the copyright page. FAIRIES AND FRIENDLY FOLK BY MARY BACON MASON

Fairies and Friendly Folk

Folk Song Pieces
For The Piano

Mary Bacon Mason

Clayton F Summy Co
Chicago   New York

Price 75 Cents

ch . . . aa, and so on—'printpaint' a vivid picture of exhaustion, almost a piece of acoustic concrete poetry." The book, in Schwartz's opinion, was "apparently the earliest important children's book where printed language is consistently used for both visual and acoustic purposes in a manner that pleasantly heightens the humor and the dynamic quality of the story."

Choo Choo is the story of a steam engine who, bored with her daily treks from town to big city, sets off on an adventure of her own. Only when a perilous downhill run ends in a dark wood on an abandoned track does she repent her rash act: "I am not going to run away any more. It isn't much fun. I'm going to pull all the coaches full of people and the baggage

They turned on
the big head light
and went slowly
up the old track.
They didn't go far before
they saw the little engine.
CHOO CHOO was so glad to be
found that she blew one "Toot"
with her whistle. There was just
enough steam left for one small "Toot".
Jim took a big chain and ran to the
little engine and hooked it on.

car from the little town to the big city and back again." Her friends — Jim the engineer, Oley the fireman, and Archibald the conductor — come to her rescue, giving Choo Choo — and readers — a happy ending.

The book, clearly a trial run for Burton, contained many elements that were refined and expanded upon in later efforts. In the first part of the story, events occur on single-page spreads, and some confusion results from train tracks that seemingly go in disparate directions. Thick and busy line work, rendered in black charcoal, tends to give a crowded look — especially in newer editions that have a smaller trim size. Burton's own hand-lettered text, replaced by type in later editions, imitated the train's motion and gave harmony to the action.

This first major effort did demonstrate what was to become a signa-

Facing page: Burton's hand-lettered text provides an intimate link between text and image; here, this informal style of lettering echoes Choo Choo's timorous cry for help. CHOO CHOO: THE STORY OF A LITTLE ENGINE WHO RAN AWAY

ture technique for her: a smooth integration of word and picture, beginning on the front cover and continuing through to the final endpapers. Burton habitually kept a sketchbook nearby, and browsing through the hundreds she filled provides revealing insights into her life and work. They offer an interesting amalgam of daily appointments, doodles, quick drawings, and concerns about her art. Tucked into one page are the words, "Do a book well or don't do it at all." Her onetime editor, Mary Silva Cosgrave, observed that "Jinnee felt keenly that the whole book was important, and she was concerned about every aspect: type, binding, jacket, title page, and endpapers."

To Burton, endpapers were integral to the process of bookmaking, as evidenced by a study of her entire work. Novels rarely had illustrated endpapers, even back then, but in *Sad-Faced Boy* she used them cleverly to set the scene.

In *Choo Choo,* Burton used the endpapers to provide a double-page panoramic setting for the upcoming story. Yellow and black railroad tracks wind through a countryside filled with neat pink-roofed houses, farmers working green fields, and cars crossing a bridge into the city over a boat-filled river. While the endpapers were rendered in sturdy colors, the story's images were in black and white.

The momentum Burton set in motion on these endpapers continued with the turn of the page. The *Horn Book* noted that the illustration created "the same kind of havoc and excitement on a large machine scale that John Gilpin did on a small horse with his famous ride in Caldecott's pen-and-ink watercolor drawings." To balance the spread, the hand-lettered title, *Choo Choo,* bends over the subtitle, *The Story of a Little Engine Who Ran Away.* Burton's name and the publisher, Houghton Mifflin,

appear in two half-circles below. (This was changed in later editions; nowadays, only the words "Choo Choo" are in Burton's own lettering.)

As she was often to do, Burton connected her life and her books. The image on the dedication page represented a scene familiar at home. In *Choo Choo,* a young boy kneels in the middle of a circular model railroad track, highlighted by a conical beam of light containing the hand-lettered words *TO MY SON ARIS*. In the background, trains from six different eras circle the page: a complete world results. In her Caldecott speech, Burton called the story "a rampant adventure of the sort that Aris often produced in miniature in his toy play."

Not until two years later would Burton again publish a book of her own. In the meantime, she contributed illustrations to a little-known

In this reverse perspective on the endpapers for *Sad-Faced Boy*, Burton first depicts a close-up of the brothers, while their friend Daisy is seen from high above; juxtaposed is the girl's point of view. The two side-by-side illustrations reflect the closed-in, canyonlike feel of the city as experienced by these rural Alabama boys.

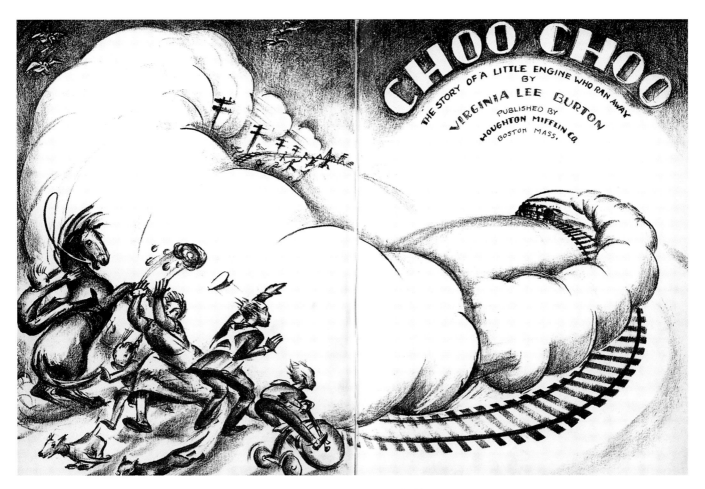

Below the title (hand lettered in this first edition), the billowing smoke and the lower-left-hand-corner frenzy set the scene for Choo Choo's adventure.

CHOO CHOO: THE STORY OF A LITTLE ENGINE WHO RAN AWAY

novel by Ethel Calvert Phillips: *Belinda and the Singing Clock*. A *Booklist* review noted that "the full-page line drawings on a brown background will not particularly appeal to the child." Neither the story nor the pictures held up; the book has long been out of print. Viewed in the context of the artist's work, however, the book provides evidence of Burton's willingness to experiment with different media, in this case scratchboard, and shows the formulation of her style.

The humble beginnings of *Mike Mulligan and His Steam Shovel* portended little of its instant popularity or its continued revered status over more than sixty years. Once again, the story was rooted in Burton's surroundings, coming simultaneously from her son Michael's beloved toy steam shovel and from Burton's observation of a nearby event: "Mary

BELINDA
and
THE SINGING CLOCK

ETHEL CALVERT PHILLIPS

With Illustrations by
VIRGINIA LEE BURTON

HOUGHTON MIFFLIN COMPANY - BOSTON
The Riverside Press Cambridge

Ann [*sic*] I found digging the cellar of the new Gloucester High School." To ensure accuracy in her illustrations, Burton visited the site regularly to watch real steam shovels in action. Burton shrewdly placed sketches of the machines on the endpapers; these diagrams are still included in hardcover editions.

The work on *Mike Mulligan* transpired over a couple of years. Burton's rigorous attention to research and detail became legendary with her editors; this perseverance, at times, caused tension when deadlines neared. "Jinnee was a perfectionist," recalls Lee Kingman Natti, "and her editors, myself included, had to almost pry final work from her hands as there

Burton's early ability to portray emotion surfaces in Belinda's delight with her birthday cake. *BELINDA AND THE SINGING CLOCK, BY ETHEL CALVERT PHILLIPS*

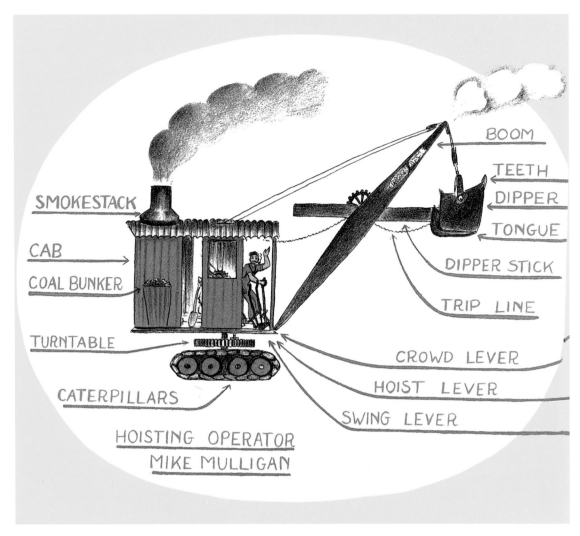

SMOKESTACK

CAB

COAL BUNKER

TURNTABLE

CATERPILLARS

HOISTING OPERATOR
MIKE MULLIGAN

BOOM

TEETH

DIPPER

TONGUE

DIPPER STICK

TRIP LINE

CROWD LEVER

HOIST LEVER

SWING LEVER

On *Mike Mulligan and His Steam Shovel*, Burton wryly commented: "The diagram of the steam shovel, with each part carefully labeled, which I put on the endpapers because I thought it too complicated and too detailed for the body of the book, aroused interest in the children."

was always one more change she wanted to make. As a result she could sometimes be very prickly."

Another factor slowing Burton's output was a personal life that overflowed with friends, home, and family. Grace Allen Hogarth, another of Burton's editors, and a longtime friend who often visited Folly Cove, told of Burton's awesome energy — especially when the children were young: "She manages to do housework, cooking, and canning, raises chickens and pigs, supervises the reluctant piano practice of her two sons, and still puts in a major part of her day on her writing and drawing. She rises at six and works before breakfast, works from breakfast until it is time to

prepare lunch, and again in the afternoon. Evenings are for darning socks, wood carving for fun, or country dancing in the barn."

Several children's illustrators of the day — Hetty Beatty, Milton Johnson, and Fen Lasell — studied with George Demetrios and were part of the Cape Ann artistic community. George and Virginia were also friends with several other prominent artists on Cape Ann — including Walker Hancock, Paul Manship, and Leon Kroll. These friendships and the sharing of artistic philosophies and techniques contributed to Burton's experimentation with art in a new way.

Facing page: Lining the walls in Burton's studio are Folly Cove curtains she designed, a wood fresco she carved, a sword used as a model in *Song of Robin Hood*, resource books and painting materials, and her ever constant record player. PHOTO BY GERDA PETERICH

In 1938 Aino Clarke, a local violinist, asked Burton to give her lessons in design; in exchange, she would teach Burton's older son, Aris, to play the violin. Other neighbors soon joined the twosome, and the design class quickly grew. Many of these people were second-generation Finns whose parents had immigrated to Cape Ann to work in the granite quarries. The class met once a week. Burton, who strongly believed that design must be a form of personal expression, insisted that her students take their designs directly from their own knowledge and interests, so many of the designs were grounded in Cape Ann life — sea and shore birds, lobstering and sailing ships, sea grasses and sea shells, blackberry bushes and morning glory flowers, and baked-bean suppers and square dances.

Over the six-month course, each person chose just one subject, which he or she was encouraged to sketch over and over to capture its essential characteristics. If, for example, a lamb were the subject, the designer would be expected not to look for a photograph but to observe a lamb itself, drawing it again and again from all positions and in its various antics until it could be fashioned with complete authority.

Burton formulated exacting homework assignments around fundamental design elements and demanded persistence and hard work. "There are no shortcuts in learning design," she said. "It is a slow and hard climb, and you never reach the top. The more you learn the more you find there is to learn."

Illustrators today echo her sentiments. Tomie dePaola, for example, states, "By the time I was a junior at Pratt Institute, it mattered, even in figure drawing, how you placed the figure on the page. Basic 2 Dimensional Design was taught with purely abstract elements, and most students, myself included, found it frustrating, a mystery, and not quite what

Burton demonstrated for her design classes how placement on the page, changes in line, and variances in black and white could alter the look of an image. FROM THE UNPUBLISHED FILES FOR *DESIGN AND HOW!*, CAPE ANN HISTORICAL ASSOCIATION

we had in mind at an art school. But that's what design is—the abstract underpinning of the image; the same way the unseen foundation of a great building holds up the structure. Good design, I believe, is timeless. It does not rely on popularism, on what is currently chic, what the 'masses' are comfortable with, or what the 'elite' raves about. Good design is usually hidden, never calling attention to itself, but supportive of the image or object it is the true foundation of."

The two ladies' dresses undergo a gradual transformation as Burton manipulated the amount of white and black in each picture. FROM THE UNPUBLISHED FILES FOR *DESIGN AND HOW!,* CAPE ANN HISTORICAL ASSOCIATION

Burton developed exercises to polish her students' skills. A subject was drawn in five tones ranging from white through gray to solid black, against backgrounds whose tones also followed the same sequence of gradations, until all possible combinations were exhausted. Then, substituting size as the variable, the process was repeated. Finally, the motif was presented in patterns of circles, squares, and rectangles, then rendered vertically, diagonally, and horizontally within those shapes, until the designer could manipulate the motif as a purely decorative element.

The philosophy Burton developed with the Folly Cove group went directly into practice in *Mike Mulligan and His Steam Shovel.* Page layout, text, and images are thoughtfully and specifically placed, and Burton's concern for pattern, repetition, spacing, and sense of movement is in evidence. Several spreads in *Mike Mulligan,* for example, show the steam from the engine paralleling puffy clouds in the sky, and the curve of the text imitating the shape of Mary Anne's cab.

The intertwining billows of white and gray smoke, the mounds of dirt unearthed from the dig, and the clutch of observers surrounding the hole all focus the eye on Mary Anne in her rightful spot at center stage.
MIKE MULLIGAN AND HIS STEAM SHOVEL

Perhaps realizing that the single-page illustrations in *Choo Choo* were insufficient for the expansiveness she wanted, Burton took advantage of the double-page spread's possibilities in *Mike Mulligan*. This larger canvas enabled Burton to accommodate the high-spirited visual movement of her work, and it eliminated the sometimes busy look of the single pages of art in *Choo Choo*.

In a particularly successful depiction, Burton details Mary Anne's finishing of the third corner of the basement. In another example, Burton melds a double-page spread with a ladder, allowing ample space for the people to climb down into the completed hole. In doing so, she gives added dimension to the event.

Burton's elegance, caught in this 1928 photograph, is also captured in the bust carved by her husband in 1936 (*bottom*). The bust is titled *Virginia Lee.* COURTESY OF THE DEMETRIOS FAMILY

Underlining the basic story lies a concern for the changing times—both cultural and mechanical—that confront Mary Anne. Burton dealt with the changes visually: automobiles share the scene with horses and buggies, and faces reflect a diversity of age and economic status—an aspect not often found in picture books of the era. Furthermore, she supplied instant personality in the bend of an old man's knee, the hunch of a child's shoulder, the gesture of a woman's hand, and the cock of a dog's head.

The notion of defining the human body in action undoubtedly derived from Burton's highly energetic life, going back to her ballet training as a teenager. She had the thin and lithe body of a dancer and a look of fragility that belied her physical and emotional strength: Grace Hogarth once called her a "fourth century B.C. Aphrodite." In her early fifties, Burton once again took dance lessons, this time from Ina Hahn, a well-known choreographer and dancer who still today lives on Cape Ann. Hahn's programs, choreographed around spatial concepts, paralleled many aspects important to Burton's design theories. The curving lines and rhythmic patterns found throughout Burton's artwork surely emanated from her love of dance.

In *Mike Mulligan,* Burton more fully developed what was to become a major theme in her work: survival through change. Through her escapade, Choo Choo learns to survive by accepting her lot in life, but in *Mike Mulligan* Burton delivered a more potent message: survival results from adapting to changes in life. It was the core of Burton's own philosophy — the need to overcome the disappointment she felt when her mother left, when she had to cancel her dancing contract to care for her father, and, later in life, when she had to adjust to her increasingly poor health.

According to Hogarth, Burton felt strongly about "the effect a book has upon a child and the responsibility that rests with the author and illustrator because of this. She points out the contrast between the German and Italian recognition of books as a means of training young minds and the scarcity of well-designed and illustrated educational books in [those countries], which are only just waking up to their opportunities for instilling a good sense of artistic values and taste as well as information.

"In each of her books there is the fundamental idea that every child comes to learn at some time — what lies behind the runaway train, the willing steam shovel, or the wistful house — and it is not always a moral. In *Choo Choo* the child learns that curiosity doesn't always pay, but he also gains the sense of responsibility that plays such a large part in his life. In *Mike Mulligan* he senses that the newest, most mechanized affairs are not always the best — that human qualities count for more — and with *The Little House,* despite all the changes of seasons and surrounds, he feels secure."

With children, however, personality is what counts, and Mary Anne fits the bill. While Mary Anne's emotions ring clear, she is mute and never

Text was in transition, the steam shovel unnamed, and illustrations not fleshed out in this early rendition of *Mike Mulligan and His Steam Shovel*.
CAPE ANN HISTORICAL ASSOCIATION

Mike Mulligan had a steam shovel
A beautiful red steam shovel
Mike Mull very big and very strong
She could dig $ds much in one day
as a 100men could dig in a week

acts outside her abilities as a steam shovel. As the catalyst for the events, she is, of course, the focus of the story and appears large and at center stage; Mike is portrayed as an adjunct to the machine. The harmony that exists between the two is supplied by sweeping curved lines in carefully spaced repetition.

An early manuscript reveals a nameless steam shovel, and in a later draft she was called Bertha, before Mary Anne finally turned up in the text. Some people speculate that the name Mary Anne was a salute to the Marion Steam Shovel Company. While the motivation behind the change is not known, the resulting alliteration and lilting ring of "Mike Mulligan and Mary Anne" surely decree that the revision was wise.

The other main character, a sturdy, blond-haired, green-overalled boy, dashes across the dedication page, bursting with enthusiasm, and later surfaces again as the one with the answer to what to do with Mary Anne. While it was Dickie Berkenbush who suggested the ingenious plot twist, it was Burton's son Michael who was the model for the boy, obviously

Nothing like this
had ever happened before
in Popperville.
Everybody started
talking at once,
and everybody had
a different idea,
and everybody thought
that his idea was the best.
They talked and they talked
and they argued and they fought
till they were worn out,
and still no one knew how to get
Mike Mulligan and Mary Anne
out of the cellar they had dug.
Then Henry B. Swap said,
'The job isn't finished because
Mary Anne isn't out of the cellar,
so Mike Mulligan won't get paid.'
And he smiled again in a rather mean way.

As in this image from *Mike Mulligan and His Steam Shovel*, Burton could deftly portray people in a variety of poses and gestures, bringing lifelike realism to her characters. Note how text follows the curve of the picture.

drawn from life. Mike is now a grown businessman in his sixties, but his proud feeling of ownership of the book shines through in conversation and is a source of constant teasing between him and his older brother.

The figures in *Mike Mulligan* explode with action. Burton renders them in an undulating style — a style that, repeated in the text, emphasizes the conflict. In today's computer-assisted world, this kind of execution could be achieved relatively easily; in 1939, it took careful synchronization between artist and typographer. Children enjoy the format elements peripherally; it is the story that engages them most. And Burton delivers it. Not only does she develop a plot that has action, emotional involvement, conflict, and a victorious ending, but she also provides a trusty heroine in Mary Anne, creates a true-blue supporting role for Mike, and rounds out the village of Popperville with a cast of appealing characters.

With the magic of her brush, Burton changed real people into book

Popperville's town hall, shown here, was modeled after the real one in West Newbury, Massachusetts, which can still be seen on Route 113. *MIKE MULLIGAN AND HIS STEAM SHOVEL*

characters. Dick Berkenbush, who was the boy who supplied the idea of what to do with Mary Anne, reports that the story's selectman, Henry B. Swap, was a combination of West Newbury storekeeper Henry Bailey and fire chief Walter Swap; the story's town constable had a striking resemblance to then town constable Willie Hudson, and the small yellow store with a sign reading SILAS ZINC, PROP. is a reference to H. Wilfred Zinc, then chairman of the West Newbury School Committee. As for Mrs. McGillicuddy, Berkenbush is sure she was patterned after somebody —but time, he says, has brushed that memory away. Berkenbush, who grew up to become the town's police and fire chief and a selectman himself, still finds time to read *Mike Mulligan* to schoolchildren in his hometown each year. His part in the ongoing success of *Mike Mulligan* continues to be an obvious pleasure.

Burton's beloved Swing Tree image appeared in various forms throughout her work. This scratch board rendition exudes the joy she found in nature. COURTESY OF CAPE ANN HISTORICAL ASSOCIATION

4 A GOLDEN MEDAL

THE EARLY 1940S WERE BURTON'S MOST FRUITFUL YEARS — SHE WROTE and illustrated three books and fashioned artwork for three others. Of the thirteen children's books she produced during her lifetime, five, including the Caldecott Medal–winning *The Little House,* were created during this time.

In those years, of course, World War II was on everyone's mind, and Virginia and George were no different. Food shortages were rampant, and gardening became not just a love but a necessity. When their plentiful plantings of beans, tomatoes, and corn became ripe, canning took precedence over deadlines. To help Virginia out, her editor Lee Kingman Natti sometimes provided a helping hand. She remembers "helping to slice basketfuls of beans on the polished granite table near the brook and boiling jars in a copper kettle over an outdoor fireplace; canning in a kitchen never held the same charm."

George's part in the war effort involved sculpting ten "average" male heads for MIT to use in developing gas masks to fit American soldiers. More than three thousand heads needed to be measured before the prototypes could be created.

With her husband commuting to Boston, Burton set herself a demanding schedule: rising at dawn, which came early on winter mornings of "doubled" daylight-saving time during the war, and working until evening, when house windows near the coastline had to be blackened for security.

Burton's books, however, dealt with themes and plots far from the ravages of war. This wasn't unusual; few children's books of that era reflected home-front deprivations, absentee fathers, or the devastation happening abroad. Other noteworthy and popular books published at the time were Robert McCloskey's *Make Way for Ducklings,* H. A. Rey's *Curious George,* and Ruth Gannett's *My Father's Dragon* — all grounded in fantasy, humor, and fun. Burton, too, lined her stories with a sense of joy and well-being. Editor Grace Allen Hogarth applauded this tactic, commenting in 1943: "In this upside-down world, children need this sense of security more than ever before."

This sense of protection and comfort was exactly what Virginia and George brought to their family life. "Looking back," son Aris says, "we never realized that others didn't live the wonderful life we did. And the fun we had! Mike and I often got into water fights when we did the dishes, and one time, in great fun and retribution, Jinnee [as they called their mother] used the air register in the floor above to drench us with a pail of water." Aris recalls that when his mother's sister came to visit, the two would dance the cha-cha around the kitchen, and that at parties he and his brother would stand near the old phonograph, stomping on the floor to make the needle jiggle. "We really pushed the envelope at times," he remembers with a wide grin.

Virginia, it seems, was less interested in punishment and more in filling their lives with the joys of living; at one point, she painted scenes from her books around the walls of their bedrooms and insisted they learn the

Facing page: Aris and Mike with their mother, whose storybook scenes — a train rolling down the tracks, romping cowboys, Mary Anne digging holes, a beaming sun — decorated her sons' bedroom walls and ceiling. STAFF/© 1944 *THE CHRISTIAN SCIENCE MONITOR*

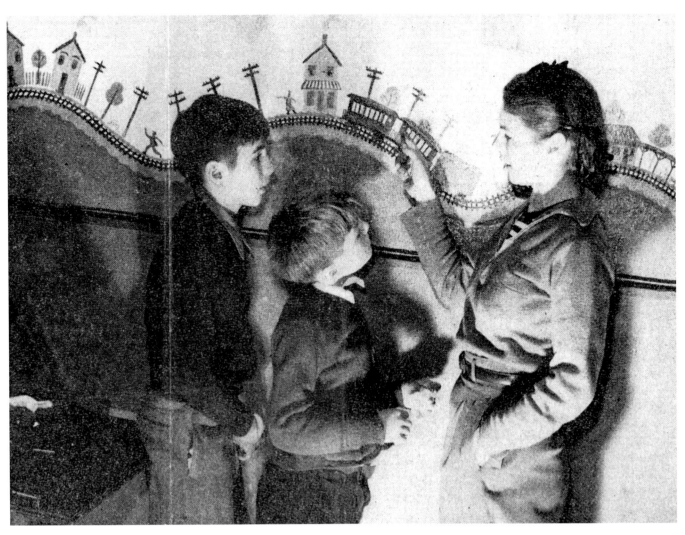

Finnish hop. Aris also tells that when a fire broke out on the second floor, his mother, home alone, lost no time in racing up the stairs with a hose to douse the flames. "She was a very resourceful woman."

Despite her familial responsibilities, Burton once again answered the call of her artistic muse. After the success of *Mike Mulligan,* she felt it was time to make a book for Aris, then nine. She started one about cars but found him unenthusiastic; he was, she said, "absorbed completely by the comics, the funnies, and radio programs." At the time, a great anti-comic-book rage gripped the country, and the idea of making a "good" comic book intrigued Burton. Eventually her thoughts evolved into *Calico the*

Wonder Horse; or, The Saga of Stewy Slinker. The plot revolves around Calico and cowboy Hank's effort to outwit the nasty desperadoes' plan to ruin a Christmas party for the children of Cactus County. It is the funniest story that Burton wrote and the only one that deviated from her major theme.

The book has an interesting history. Burton began with the wish to wean her children away from the highly popular comic books. She said, "I really dislike the comic books for their lack of design and drawing more than anything; however, I did let them listen to the Lone Ranger on the radio. I am afraid I was 'spoofing' all Westerns. I still can't hear the Overture to William Tell without saying 'Hi O Silver.'"

As before, Burton began with research. From her study of comic books she concluded that "the hero must be endowed with more than the average physical and mental powers, besides being all that was chivalrous and virtuous, and the villain the antithesis. There must be action, suspense, and tremendous but possible odds against the hero, but no one must get seriously hurt. Humor was welcome." After discovering the Old West saying, "When in doubt, trust to yo' hoss," which she later said was her cue, she made the central character a horse.

After sketching out the characters and plot, Burton took the story to her publisher, where Grace Hogarth had just taken over as juvenile editor. Later Burton would comment, *"Calico* was an experiment and a risk for any publisher, but despite all this, Grace encouraged me, gave me a free hand, and in a sense fostered the book into existence." In one aspect, however, Burton was not given a free hand: she had originally named the bad guy Stewy Stinker but, at the urging of several librarians, it was changed to Slinker, much to Burton's chagrin.

The book was published on poor-grade wartime paper in a rainbow of

Facing page: In making her horse, Calico, female, Burton felt she was giving a tongue-in-cheek poke to Western comics, where women were mostly ignored. Here, diminishing-in-size cacti and radiating sun spikes effectively spotlight the pony. CALICO THE WONDER HORSE

Way out West in Cactus County there was a horse named Calico. She wasn't very pretty . . . but she was very smart. She was the smartest fastest horse in all of Cactus County.

colors, resembling the writing tablets popular with children at the time. The rainbow effect was, according to Burton, the publisher's idea, and one that she welcomed. "I could make the drawings in black and get the two-color effect the children liked." The background colors also helped to support the story: a soft pastel green echoes the quiet life in Cactus County; when the scene shifts to the Bad Lands, the color is a more vibrant lavender; blacks, always the heaviest for the Bad Men, give a sinister effect; and the capture of Stewy Slinker is in light brown, his escape in pale green. Cerise and brilliant orange bring the story to its climax; blue, with a violent storm, starts the *dénouement;* and a soft, warm yellow envelops the happy ending.

Unhappy with some of the original illustrations, Burton welcomed the

Stewy Slinker drove the stagecoach down the narrow mountain road at a breakneck speed. Hank and Calico were fast behind and the stampede thundering after them.

Examination of two scenes from the 1941 original (*top*), and the 1951 revision (*bottom*), in *Calico* demonstrate how addition of detail, better use of space, and sharper delineation between black and white energize and individualize a picture. *CALICO THE WONDER HORSE*

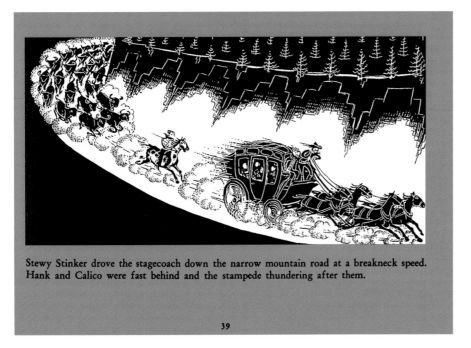

Stewy Stinker drove the stagecoach down the narrow mountain road at a breakneck speed. Hank and Calico were fast behind and the stampede thundering after them.

39

opportunity, in 1950, to make new drawings, which she injected with more action. In addition to fine-tuning the story, she defined the backgrounds, enlivened the faces, and added more design elements. And, most important, she finally got her way about the bad guy's name: Stinker was reinstated and remains to this day.

In this WANTED poster from the 1951 revision, Burton makes sly reference to a change she had long lobbied for — *Slinker* to *Stinker*. CALICO THE WONDER HORSE

The 1997 paperback reprint displayed a slight change of color pattern, but it still maintains Burton's ambience. Also included in this version is a publisher's note that talks briefly about the book's history. After being out of print for many years, *Calico* again offers readers a fun tale of high jinks and adventure.

At the time of publication, the book received mixed reviews. *Parents* magazine found it "an experimental — and unusual — book that meets the sensational comics on their own ground." Reviewer L. Felix Ranlett, on the other hand, claimed the book lacked the "gusto" of other Burton books, complaining that the color device did not "do away with the obscurity of too much black." As for the humor, he says, "we suspect that some-

Then the fireworks started. Hi! Yi! Whoopee! High went Calico and hard she hit.

Calico bounded down the mountainside leaping from rock to rock like a jack-rabbit. Stewy Stinker pulled leather so hard he got calluses on both hands.

Two whoops and a holler and they were over the river. Lightning was slow in comparison to the way they covered the country . . .

back to Hank who was waiting. Calico stopped short and unloaded Stewy Stinker

18

19

body is being kidded. Could it be us? We like our funnies and our books kept separate and we don't know whether *Calico* is a book or a funny."

Critic Barbara Bader has a different vision. In her retrospective study *American Picturebooks from Noah's Ark to the Beast Within,* she states that *Calico* is not a comic book at all, but a takeoff on comic books. "The illustrations have more in common with the strip silhouettes of Caran d'Ache, the nineteenth-century French comic illustrator, than with the crypto-naturalism of contemporary comics."

Burton gave Hank, young enough to have been her older son, a spirited horse named Calico and pitted not one but five rogues against the pair, with the chief scoundrel being Stewy. She relates, "I made Stewy Stinker and his Bad Men—Butch Bones, Snake Eye Pyezon, Buzzard Bates, and little Skunk Skeeter—both villainous and comic, and got them into the most ridiculous positions the boys and I could contrive. We laid the scene in Cactus County with the Bad Lands over the river."

Eventually dubbed a "symphony in comics" by her family, the book clearly reflects Burton's emphasis on movement. Her comments about the artwork indicate her evolving thoughts. "In design, movement is opposed to monotony. The circle or half-circle is at rest. Developed into a spiral, it moves. A right angle is stationary. A slight variation in degree

Using the comic book format to full effect, Burton doubles the humor as Calico takes Stewy on a wild ride before throwing him into a cactus bush at Hank's feet. *CALICO THE WONDER HORSE*

and it immediately takes on life. Calico's and Hank's theme in action produces wave-like spirals that sweep through the book to end at last in a quiet half-circle, complete repose, and peace."

Burton was not the only illustrator to use high-quality pictures in comic-book form to tell a funny story. Earlier, Nikolay Radlov produced *The Cautious Carp* (1938) and, six years after *Calico,* illustrator Helen Sewell, who was also concerned about the slipshod techniques of comics, created *Three Tall Tales.* However, as Cornelia Meigs said in *A Critical History of Children's Literature,* "None of these artists could compete with the availability of the comics, for the production costs of a well-drawn and well-produced book could not approach the cheapness of the comic book." This idea holds even today; while British illustrator Marcia Williams has interpreted a number of classics in comic-book format, Avi and Brian Floca have experimented with the form in the novel *City of Light, City of Darkness,* and Loreen Leedy has played with the technique in several of her math books, it is not often seen in today's trade books.

On the heels of *Calico,* Burton created illustrations for Leigh Peck's *Don Coyote* and Arna Bontemps and Jack Conroy's *The Fast Sooner Hound,* her second collaboration with Bontemps. Another book she worked on presents something of a puzzle: Kenneth Henderson's *Manual of American Mountaineering,* written for an adult audience, was published by the American Alpine Club in 1941, but when a version of the book was issued in 1942 by Burton's publisher, Houghton Mifflin, under the title *Handbook of American Mountaineering,* Burton was given no illustration credit. Burton's nephew, Costa Maletskos, who spent many summers with the Demetrios family, recalls Burton agonizing over the illustrations for rappelling, belaying, and knot tying, but has no explanation for why she

18   AMERICAN MOUNTAINEERING

Figure 29. Use of Handhold that Improves on Ascending

Although Burton is not credited for the illustrations in *Manual of American Mountaineering,* the mobility of the figures indicates she did the work.
HOUGHTON MIFFLIN COMPANY

them to say which of us really has a bad nose. We must get the question settled. We can't go on quarrelling like this day after day and night after night.'

Queen Leona agreed, and King Léon ordered the crows to carry his message. All the animals were told to come that very evening to the royal cave. At sundown they began to arrive; and by the time the moon rose all were there — the Bear, the Wolf, the Burro, the Goat, the Rattlesnake, the Fox, the Pole Cat, the Paisano, the Armadillo, the Sheep, the wild Mustang, the Coyote, and many others.

'You are called here,' King Léon announced, 'to decide an important question. It has been charged, on the one hand, that my own royal nose smells bad, and,

on the other hand, that it is the nose of Queen Leona which offends. Will one of you volunteer to smell the noses of both of us and say which one is ill-smelling?'

Burro stepped forward immediately, eager to take an important part. Bowing politely to the royal couple, he smelled first the nose of the Lion and then that of the Lioness.

Señor Burro was a gallant fellow who liked to please the ladies. Nobody was surprised when he decided, 'The fault must be with King Léon. Charming Queen Leona could never give offense.' And he smiled at her.

wasn't listed as the illustrator. In comparing the two books, it is obvious that the work is Burton's.

Don Coyote, a southwestern folktale, incorporated stories about Coyote, a champion of the underdog, who enjoys taking advantage of the stupidity of other animals, just for the fun of it, and sometimes gets fooled in the process. The title page finds Coyote in high action, tail up, head thrust forward, legs in motion. While some of the small "still life" vignettes are less successful, the action scenes are full of verve and emotion.

Bontemps, pleased with Burton's renditions for *Sad-Faced Boy,* requested that she provide the art for *The Fast Sooner Hound,* a tall tale about Boomer, a railroad engineer, and his dog, Sooner, who runs so fast that he outraces

Here, Burton rings the text with a collection of animals in graduated sizes, topped off by two lions sitting effectively and gracefully in repose. In contrast, the double-page spread (*right*) is an action-filled extravaganza. DON COYOTE BY LEIGH PECK

of the young Blackbirds even, doing loops and nose dives and tail spins. All these tricks put a severe strain on his newly implanted feathers, which before long began to pull loose and give way.

'Help, help,' Coyote cried. 'I'm falling!'

But the Blackbirds were ahead of him now, and were making so much noise with their cries to each other that they could not hear Coyote's call for help.

For a moment he thought he could not possibly save himself from crashing into a pile of rocks. Then, as he directed his course away from the rocks, he saw that he was headed toward a clump of Spanish Daggers, ready to impale him on their long thorns. But, by a last effort

68

of his failing wings, he managed to direct his fall toward a juniper thicket.

The sweet-smelling juniper branches broke his fall, but even so, he hit with a thud that knocked the breath out of him. When at last he got it back and convinced himself that he had no bones broken, Coyote found that his plumage was all gone, except for a few shrivelled feathers along his forelegs and on the tip of his tail.

To this day, Coyote pups are often born with little black fringes of hair on their forelegs and with black tail-tips.

the Cannon Ball Express. In preparing the illustrations, Burton acutely felt the restrictions of the page, and told her editor that this was the last book she would work on that she didn't write. According to editor Natti, Burton was "dismayed by the amount of type in proportion to illustration, and from then on she was not interested in illustrating any book in which she could not control the length of the text."

Nevertheless, her pictures for the book are superb; a more energetic, ecstatic canine would be hard to find, and she cleverly utilized the page, giving the tale great visual dynamics. On the title page, a symbolic treatment foreshadows a triumphant Sooner leaping over a much smaller train in the distance. As the story ends, true friends Sooner and Boomer ride

Just before the starting whistle blew, the Roadmaster climbed into the cab of the Cannon Ball with the Boomer and the Engineer. He wanted to be sure that the Boomer shoveled plenty of coal and that the Engineer kept the fast train moving at top speed. He also wanted to be close at hand to laugh at the Boomer when the Cannon Ball pulled away from the old lop-eared Sooner.

A clear track for a hundred miles was ordered for the Cannon Ball, and all the switches were spiked down. The train pulled out of the station like a streak of lightning. It took three men to see the Cannon Ball pass on that run: one to say, "There she comes," one to say, "Here she is," and another to say, "There she goes." You couldn't see a thing for steam, cinders, and smoke. The rails sang like a violin for half an hour after she had passed into the next county.

18

off on the train together—again bringing Burton's theme of survival to the forefront.

These books published in the early 1940s foretell the design elements that Burton was to use in her most prestigious book, *The Little House,* for which she won the 1943 Caldecott Medal.

Part of that book's success undoubtedly derived from the influence of Burton's work with the Folly Cove group, which had been an informal but continual part of her life. As the number of her students increased and their work became more professional, it was time, Burton thought, to hold their first exhibition. In the summer of 1940, her studio was turned into an art gallery to display their fabric items (draperies, table linens, and clothing) and paper products (wallpaper, stationery, and greeting cards).

Just as Burton's books reflected her concern about aesthetic elements lost to the industrial era, so did her work with Folly Cove. In an article in *Country Gentleman,* she noted: "Back at the beginning of the Machine Age the designer and craftsman got separated. The designer became white

Facing page: Burton pulls the reader directly into the story with a train that zooms across the page in a swish of color and a hound, ears flying, that gallops alongside, puffs of dirt disappearing in his wake. THE FAST SOONER HOUND BY ARNA BONTEMPS AND JACK CONROY

collar. The craftsman became a superior sort of mechanic. We [Folly Cove Designers] not only learn to draw, and to carve our drawings into linoleum blocks; we follow the job straight through. Nobody's afraid to get a little ink on his or her hands. Nobody's afraid to be a craftsman as well as a designer."

The class concentrated on the elements of design — size, pattern, repetition, shape, and spacing — and they worked tirelessly to meet Burton's high standards. They immediately elected officers, and while Burton refused the title of president, she was always the unofficial leader.

The design elements that Burton taught to the group are clearly evident in *The Little House*: the presentation of the trees, the semicircles of suns, the landscape spirals, and the sweep of roads that cross the page. The idea for the book had been germinating in Burton's mind for many years before it began to appear on paper. Archival material reveals some of the process: one early sketch indicates, for example, that the original title was "The Little Pink House." And original printer's dummies show how text was cut out, shaped into a block, and precisely placed. Similarly, the arches that cross the sky (seen in suns and stars) were painted individually, cut out, and strategically positioned on the page.

In 1932, when Burton and her husband purchased their house in Folly Cove, they moved the building back away from the road and traffic noise and planted a whole field of daisies, Burton's favorite flower. The experience of this move and what it represented to Burton were the book's focus. The house itself, somewhat larger today after the addition of a wing following a fire, was a small, two-storied, slant-roofed building, with gray shingles and lemon-colored shutters; it is not the pink Cape Cod dwelling of the book.

On the page, the Little House is cozily shaped, deliberately personifying rural Americana and emphasizing the building's survival through decades of change. The country setting and the portrayal of the cycle of the seasons reflected Burton's surroundings. The swing tree, so meaningful to Burton and used in her Folly Cove designs, in a 1965 *Horn Book* calendar, and in *Life Story,* appears first in *The Little House.* She used the swing tree often—not only placing her husband, her sons, and herself, complete with drawing pad, in the scene, but also inserting friends and family—to make a life-to-book connection. The rhythmic patterns and the variation of color tones that Burton wove into the spreads both quickens and moderates the pace, reinforcing her seamless story.

As with all her books, Burton began *The Little House* by drawing the pictures first, although, said editor Natti, the story line was already in her head. The completed sketches were pinned in sequence on her studio walls, allowing her to see the book as a whole. After preparing a rough dummy, she then typed out the words and placed them in aesthetic and previously designated spaces. Whenever possible, text was eliminated and pictures changed to allow a more visual presentation of the tale.

In the preparation stage, Burton lured her children and their friends with cookies and cocoa to listen to the story until she was satisfied that it thoroughly captivated their interest. Often, Burton said, "they [Aris and Michael] were responsible for changing the ending of a story." She felt that this constant contact with her audience removed the temptation to "write down" to children and that it resulted in a tighter integration of pictures and text.

The work on *The Little House* didn't always go smoothly, and at one point she was "ready to junk" the project. The difficulty she faced was to

An early depiction of the Little House appeared first in this form in one of Burton's sketchbooks. CAPE ANN HISTORICAL ASSOCIATION

"convey the idea of historical perspective, or the passage of time, in terms comprehensible to a child." She solved the problem, she said in her Caldecott speech, in this way: "The rising and setting of the sun signify the passing of the hours of the day; the waxing and waning of the moon, the succession of the days of the month; and the rotations of the seasons, the evanescence of the year." She felt that once this rhythm was established, the child would grasp the idea of change and perspective. Indeed, in the final product, she handled it admirably: color, detail, and pattern allow the child to conceive of a century of growth, while the interspersed nocturnal scenes bring relief to the bright colors and help to accentuate the flow of time.

Burton's signature sprawling ovals and ovals within ovals — in the clouds, fields, roads, fences, and treetops — portray an idyllic world of springtime splendor and exemplify her creative use of design principles. *THE LITTLE HOUSE*

The circular patterns that flow through the first thirteen pages, shaped to fit the page, suggest the harmonious values of country life. When change occurs, diagonal lines and drab grays and browns portend the coming industrialization. Roads slash through the countryside, trucks belch smoke, vehicles crowd the roads, elevated trains rush by, buildings tower above, and people jam the streets. Soon, the Little House is forgotten. The curtained windows, which once personified a face full of contentment, are boarded over, and a now-smudged exterior sags with lines of despair. The final five pages, showing the Little House's return to the country, bring back the lighter colors and curved images.

Daytime in the country shines with light pastel colors, while daylight city scenes feature darker colors. Once again Burton's sketchbooks hint at her evolving thoughts. "Composition — House in same spot changing

Gray clouds on the horizon, road-building equipment on the scene, and a ROAD CLOSED sign in the foreground enhance the Little House's apprehensive appearance, cleverly foretelling events to come. *THE LITTLE HOUSE*

surroundings—first in color, then in buildings. Little extra things going on inside the big composition."

Burton deftly used format to vary the pace: country scenes appear on single pages, while city images sprawl across double pages, with single pages reappearing once the city is left behind. This change is instituted gradually and inventively. The early pages are decorated with symbolic motifs (birds, suns, daisies, and snowflakes), and then, slowly, small vignettes appear, subtly connected to an illustration. Finally, the illustration expands into a two-page spread. The shape of the text changes in tandem: gentle curves depict the "tranquility of the country," while structured text blocks characterize the disorder of the city, where "everyone seemed in such a hurry."

Burton drew on the plot's inherent drama, enticing readers to look for

Dark colors and frenzied activity convey the mood of the Little House at the height of her despair. *THE LITTLE HOUSE*

the many specific events in the pictures: the sight of a Mike and Mary Anne lookalike (page 15 of the book); the changing countryside; the reappearing images (children skinny-dipping in summer, skating in winter; men working the fields; horse-drawn carriages prancing down the road); and objects disappearing over the years (the pond, trees, and horses). Readers also delight in the endpapers (seen in the hardcover edition), which wryly trace the history of transportation and subtly underscore the ironies to follow. Burton tells that, knowing children's delight in this kind of detail, she deliberately gave one car a flat tire to see if her children would notice: they did.

In allowing her heroine to escape the urban chaos, Burton embodied a theme common in American literature and left the Little House with the values she treasured in her earlier pastoral environment. When asked

At the close, Burton signals the happier mood of the story's beginning with a doorstep that curves into a smile, pink flowering trees, sunny skies, and children once again playing in the yard.

THE LITTLE HOUSE

Once again
she was lived in
and taken care of.

if the story's point was that the further away we get from nature and the simple way of life the less happy we are, Burton said that she was "quite willing to let this be its message."

The book is an excellent study for many reasons. It gives a glimpse into Burton's personal life, it conceptualizes her philosophy of living in harmony with nature, it exemplifies the further development of her major theme, it shows her use of design elements, and it is a splendid example of a seamless picture book that works on many levels.

With *The Little House,* Burton reached the pinnacle of her picture-book work: *Choo Choo* is an entertaining but somewhat bland adventure; *Mike Mulligan,* although the most popular, is not as artistically sound; *Calico* is funny but experimental. Those to come—*Katy* and *Maybelle*—don't have the energy of *The Little House; Song of Robin Hood,* an artistic tour de force, and *Life Story,* an amazing well of information, lack *The Little House*'s child appeal. It was a wise choice for the Caldecott Medal, as it embodies for the child, the critic, the teacher, and the adult reader all that a picture book can and should be.

There was one downside to the success of *The Little House.* Walt Disney personally invited Burton to California to talk about making a film of the Caldecott Medal–winning book, royally wining and dining her, but to obtain the actual license, Disney negotiated directly with Houghton Mifflin's subrights and permissions office, which granted Disney the film rights for a mere $1,000. Burton was unhappy with the settlement. When the film was released in 1951, Burton's displeasure increased: the images and text were completely changed from her original work—even the structure of the house was altered—and she felt that using a bride and groom at the story's beginning and end moved it beyond the young audience she had worked so hard to capture. (Bill Peet, then a Disney cartoonist, was the book's adapter; in his autobiography, he called *The Little House* "a gem of a book.")

In her book *Art and Design in Children's Picture Books,* Lyn Lacy compares *The Little House* to Maurice Sendak's *Where the Wild Things Are* and to Chris Van Allsburg's *Jumanji,* pointing to the trio as excellent examples of how book design contributes to the idea behind the story. The opening page of *The Little House,* she says, "is a perfect presentation of text designed to fit within an illustration or the imposition of words into a field of action to balance the overall composition," but she criticizes Burton's ending, saying that using a single page rather than a double-page spread was disappointing. However, it seems equally viable that Burton's intention was to complete the circle, so to speak, repeating the depiction

Facing page: The Little House as portrayed in the 1951 Disney film adaptation. BILL PEET: AN AUTOBIOGRAPHY BY BILL PEET

of the first page and bringing readers back to their original view of the Little House. In the end, the narrative reads: "Once again she was lived in and taken care of," leaving the same satisfying feeling that Maurice Sendak brings to *Where the Wild Things Are* with its final observation about Max's supper: "and it was still hot."

In a review published in the *New York Times Book Review* prior to its receiving the Caldecott Medal, Anne Eaton said that *The Little House* had "lively imagination and genuine power," stating that Burton had made "an original and charming picture book that tells in absorbing fashion what happens as cities grow larger." In a recent article in the *Seattle Times,* Nicole Brodeur called *The Little House* a cautionary tale about urban sprawl and urged builders to keep it on their nightstands.

Though few dates are found in Burton's sketchbooks, one page has an undoubted reference to her Caldecott speech: "Speech due June 8, Spoken–Read June 14." Notes that follow include: "Idea, children's books.

Why I write them—every book different—technique. Learn something every time. Little House—history. Time—sun moon seasons, periods."

Due to travel restrictions placed on civilians during World War II, the American Library Association canceled its 1943 convention. Nevertheless, New York State librarians organized a festive occasion at the Hotel Roose-

Facing page: In her 1943 Caldecott speech, Burton said, "The changing surroundings represent the sweep of social history; or to make a very bad pun, 'her story.'" Those words protrude from the front doorstep of the Little House, an unintended message, perhaps, to future feminists who would claim those words as a suitable substitution for *"history."*

velt in New York City on June 14 at which the Newbery and Caldecott awards were presented. Arrangements were also made for NBC to broadcast the program over the radio. Since Burton lived in Massachusetts, and Elizabeth Janet Gray, who received the Newbery Medal that year for *Adam of the Road,* resided in Philadelphia, both were able to attend. Information does not indicate whether or not Caldecott honorees Mary and Conrad Buff (for *Dash and Dart*) and Clare Turlay Newberry (for *Marshmallow*) were in attendance. It is interesting to note, however, that both honor books reflect the pastoral theme found in *The Little House.*

The presentation fell on Flag Day, and with patriotism in 1943 at a high, a special point was made to celebrate that holiday, as well as the twenty-fifth anniversary of Children's Book Week. Sharing the dais that evening were ALA president Keyes Metcalf, from Harvard; Frederick G. Melcher, publisher and sponsor of the Newbery and Caldecott awards; Lillian Smith, president of the Children's Library Association and head of children's services at the Toronto Public Library; Harriet Long, of Case Western Reserve, chair of the Newbery/Caldecott Committee; and Anne Carroll Moore, head of children's work at the New York Public Library. As part of her remarks, Moore, known for her harsh criticism, credited Burton with making "an honest-to-goodness American picture book."

Burton, who spoke that night about her career and the genesis of several of her books, ended her Caldecott speech with these thoughtful words: "The basic things are always the most important, and good art, certainly a basic thing, impressed on young minds through the medium of children's books, is without doubt one of the best possible ways of giving children a true conception of the world they live in."

"Dance of the Hours" by Virginia Lee Demetrios

5 FOLLY COVE DESIGNERS

Burton and her fellow Folly Cove Design craftsmen created another world, more for adults than for children, in their innovative designs, some of which had a definite storytelling aspect. Their first exhibition, in 1940, drew more than 150 people and included tablecloths, kerchiefs, scarves, and handkerchiefs, some in color and some in black and white. The *Gloucester Daily Times* heralded the show: "The designs evolved by the 'graduates,' most of whom never previously studied art, are receiving the praise of highly rated artists and decorators."

"Sauna," a Finnish-inspired, dark-blue-on-white design by Burton's friend Aino Clarke, who had set the whole enterprise rolling, received particular attention. The group's success was heady, and they were ever diligent about keeping their standards high. When they decided to organize professionally, the chosen name sprang naturally from the area that inspired much of their work: Folly Cove Designers. By 1945, more than 500 people were attending the exhibitions to admire and purchase designs new and old and, by tradition, to sip strong coffee and nibble on Finnish bread, called *nisu*. Encouraged, the designers began selling their goods to the general public. Before long, the Folly Cove Designers were being lauded across the country and even internationally as nearby hotels rec-

ommended the shop to guests, and overseas visitors sent their friends at home samples of these unique American crafts.

Later that year, Burton and several group members traveled to New York to visit America House, a retail outlet for national crafts. Established by the American Craftsman Cooperative Council, America House was formed in response to a revival of the arts and crafts movement that occurred in America in the late 1930s and early 1940s.

Representatives, headed by Frances Wright (daughter of Frank Lloyd Wright), accepted the designers' work for retail sale; for several years, America House became one of their largest wholesale customers. The trip also included a stop at Macy's department store, where a buyer, while

Heart-shaped branches cleverly help shape Burton's tree designs for her unique display of the seasons. "SWING TREE II," CAPE ANN HISTORICAL ASSOCIATION

enthusiastic about their work, suggested that sales would benefit from more streamlined production methods. She told Burton, "You could be driving a Rolls Royce instead of a Ford." Burton replied, "I like my Ford." This exchange tellingly revealed Burton's homespun attitude about life and about art—one that plays out in many of her children's stories.

Always concerned with being impartial in this close circle of friends

A colorful array of Folly Cove fabrics, individually designed, cut, and printed from linoleum blocks, would await customers each summer; some blocks took nearly eighty hours to carve.
HOUGHTON MIFFLIN COMPANY ARCHIVES

and family, the Folly Cove Designers decided, in 1943, to form a rotating jury, to be made up of the group's senior members; both Virginia Lee Burton and George Demetrios served regularly. The rivalries and infighting that often begin in this kind of enterprise never happened with the Folly Cove Designers. The emphasis was on the work, not the individual. According to onetime designer Mary Ann Lash: "We enjoyed each other as craftsmen and as people. We were given the opportunity to be creative, which was a unique and welcome factor here at Folly Cove for people who love simplicity and the natural world. Also, each person respected the others' work, and each person gave and took away from the class. But especially it was Jinnee—her sensitivity to nature and her recognition of people's creativity—that bound us together somehow."

Not only did candidates desiring membership in the Folly Cove Designers need to complete Burton's design course, but they also had to submit a design for jury approval. A design was not approved until it was deemed to represent the best work the designer could do at the time; popular appeal was not enough. Their mutual insistence on quality proved worthwhile: the designers participated in the Exhibition of Contemporary New England Handicrafts at the Worcester Art Museum. It was the first of more than fifteen museum showings they enjoyed in the 1940s and 1950s.

As word spread about the high quality and uniqueness of the Folly Cove work, a need surfaced for someone to handle the group's business affairs. Dorothy Norton, one of the designers, took on that responsibility. She established wholesale and retail prices and made arrangements for each designer to receive a proportionate compensation.

Over the twenty-five years of their operation, forty-three individuals

Facing page: "A Fish Story" by Virginia Lee Demetrios, 1957

were certified as Folly Cove Designers. But because of job changes, career commitments, and World War II living adjustments, only about fifteen to eighteen contributed at any one time. Burton's younger brother, Ross, a silversmith by trade, and his wife were active until they moved away from the area. In the course of time, 333 designs were accepted by the five-member jury. "And that," said Norton, "means a lot of linoleum."

Linoleum was, of course, the material of choice for preparing the printing blocks. While preliminary designs were scratched into the black ink that had been applied to white cardboard, final works were executed on

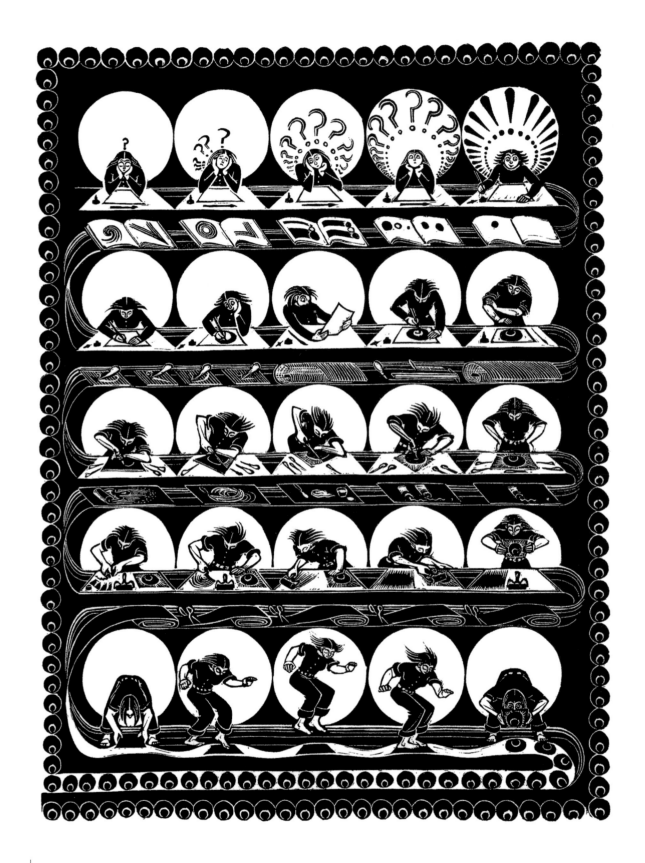

Facing page: Burton presented this piece to each graduate of her design classes; nicknamed "The Diploma," it traces the creative process from idea to finished product and is graced with her keen sense of composition as well as her flair for humor. *FOLLY COVE DESIGNER BY VIRGINIA LEE DEMETRIOS*

linoleum covered with gesso or white shoe polish. After the design was drawn on, a mat knife was used to cut away the white parts, and each edge was beveled to withstand the pressure of printing. Carving a block could take eighty hours or more, depending on the complexity of the design. Once the carving was finished, any color to be incorporated was added—each with a separate printing—using a gum roller. Imprinting the designs entailed laying the blocks on fabric or paper, inked side down, and stamping on them with bare feet. Later, hand-operated presses made the job much easier and faster. The Folly Cove Designers used acorn presses, which had Gothic arches and a strong, simple structure. Since presses of this type were not made after 1865, most of them were well over a hundred years old; however, the designers found them efficient as well as decorative. During the war years, a more troubling problem was the unreliability of inks, until the U.S. Navy's research into water- and sun-proof inks yielded a better product.

A new and exciting breakthrough occurred in 1944 when the department store Lord & Taylor purchased rights to five of the designs. One, called "Gossips," signed Virginia Lee Demetrios (she used her married name in all her Folly Cove work), is an amusing study in over-the-back-yard-fence communication and evokes the same small-town-America feeling as a 1948 illustration by Norman Rockwell also entitled *The Gossips*.

According to an article in the *New York Times,* buyers at Lord & Taylor believed that the Folly Cove patterns represented a "new direction" in fabric design. They had the designs printed on cotton twill, using a screen-printing process that was "modified to retain some of the imperfections typical of hand prints." To showcase these new offerings, the store featured the fabrics in its Fifth Avenue windows and in interior store settings

Eino Natti, one of the few men involved in the Folly Cove Designers, inks a linoleum block for printing on their acorn press, seen on the left.
HOUGHTON MIFFLIN COMPANY ARCHIVES

and ran full-page ads in the *Boston Transcript* and the *New York Times*.

By happenstance, a popular syndicated columnist of the time, Roger Babson, saw the Lord & Taylor displays and, having grown up in Glouces-ter, was particularly intrigued. The story he wrote for the *Washington Post* about the Folly Cove Designers appeared in more than 400 newspapers across the country. This bit of serendipity led to another: U.S. Congres-sional Representative Jerry Voorhis of California, seeing the *Post* article, requested that Babson's piece be read into the *Congressional Record* as an example of "a thriving and successful cooperative enterprise, operating in a manner similar to the old medieval guilds." And, as one piece of pub-licity often spawns others, *Life, Magazine Digest,* the *Boston Herald, Coun-try Gentleman, Craft Horizons,* and *Yankee* soon delivered their own editorial spins. Soon, these twenty-five men and women were making a difference not just in their small community but across the country as well. *Life* mag-azine ran a four-page article about the designers, heralding their work

Facing page: Life brought national attention to the small craft guild on Cape Ann; eventually, however, that recognition became a burden and led to their disbandment. *LIFE,* NOVEMBER 26, 1945.
PHOTOGRAPHS BY HAROLD CARTER

with close-up photos and showcasing five of their designs. Commercial businesses such as F. Schumacher, Rich's department store in Atlanta, and Skinner Silks commissioned special themes, as did the Guernsey Society of America, Smith College, and Old Sturbridge Village. Before long, more than thirty retail stores were carrying Folly Cove Designs.

As their fame grew, so did the group's need for a larger space. In 1948, the Folly Cove Designers opened their own headquarters in an old barn on Washington Street. The exhibitions attracted hundreds of people who

VIRGINIA DEMETRIOS (STANDING) WEARS HER OWN SPRING-LAMB PRINT AT A FOLLY COVE DESIGNERS' MEETING

FOLLY COVE DESIGNERS
YANKEE PRINTS GET NATIONAL RECOGNITION

A new series of fabrics with a distinctly Yankee flavor will soon be on sale in at least 14 leading department stores throughout the country, thus bringing national recognition to the modest Folly Cove Designers of Cape Ann, Mass. This is a group of young married women who five years ago started to make hand-blocked prints in their spare time. They drew the scenes and people around them,

did all their work by hand, as shown in pictures on these pages, and produced the quaint and humorous prints on pages 82 and 83. Several months ago six designs were bought for screen-printing in large quantities. The Folly Cove Designers operates as a guild. Every design, before being accepted, must be approved by a jury of five members and the group gets a percentage of the profits.

FIRST STEP is making a sketch. Here Louise Kenyon sketches "Head of the Cove" (top opposite page).

WHITE PAINT is spread over a block from which the design will be cut. This makes it easier to see design.

DESIGN IS DRAWN with a brush or a pencil on the white-painted block, after it is completely dry.

LIFTING THE BLOCK OFF THE FABRIC IS THE FINAL STEP. THIS "HEAD OF THE COVE" PRINT IS SHOWN ON PAGE 83

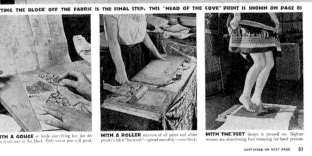

WITH A GOUGE or knife everything but the design is cut out of the block. Only uncut part will print.

WITH A ROLLER mixture of oil paint and white printer's ink is "buttered"—spread smoothly—over block.

WITH THE FEET design is pressed on. Slighter women are abandoning foot stamping for hand presses.

80

CONTINUED ON NEXT PAGE   81

came to see the demonstrations and buy the products. Visiting the barn, according to Mary Ann Lash, was always a delight. The colorful and beautifully designed fabrics hung from the ceiling, and tables, decorated with pots of flowers, displayed a variety of place mats, runners, tablecloths, cocktail napkins, guest towels, baby bibs, pinafores, and greeting cards. Except for a mailing list of established customers, the Folly Cove Designers did not advertise; nevertheless, their popularity continued to grow. Originally open just in August, the barn was eventually winterized, allowing expanded hours from March through December. Prior to the March opening, the designers all pitched in to help get ready: one archival photo

Facing page: "Kitnip" by Virginia Lee
Demetrios, 1949

shows Burton herself on her knees, scrubbing the floor. All this care paid off, as each year approximately $13,000 was distributed among the designers. Burton was one of the top producers.

Burton's designs, illustrations, paintings, and wood carvings were drawn from a deep artistic well and from a close intertwining of her art and personal life. Among the designs she created for Folly Cove, "George's Garden" shows her love of gardening; "Fish Story," her delight in the sea; "Kitnip" and "Spring Lambs I and II," her affection for animals; and "Grand Right and Left," her joy in square dancing. Some patterns are seeded in her books: "The Little House," "Robin Hood," and "Choo Choo" are obvious, but connections can also be found in "Commuting" and "Gloucester Branch," built around train motifs, and in "Swing Tree," an image that figures prominently in *Life Story*. And since Burton's sense of fun is continually pointed out by those who knew her, designs such as "Gossips," "Reducing," and "Folly Cove Designer" provide a ready indication of her wit and effervescent personality. Another of Burton's more famous blocks was "Zaidee and Her Kittens," named after the perpetually pregnant family cat. By necessity, Burton continually looked for homes for Zaidee's offspring and as incentive would present a set of printed "Zaidee" place mats to the fortunate new owner.

In the mid-sixties, Burton's growing health problems undermined her usual energetic inspiration. Furthermore, the demand for products became "too much; it began to devour the rest of their lives" according to Folly Cove historian Pat Earle. From 1941 to 1955 the group participated in sixteen museum exhibits and found their designs in thirty retail stores. Then, when Burton died in 1968, the light of the Folly Cove Designers went out. Without their mentor and creative muse, the designers decided to close their doors and cease operations. They agreed never to sell any of the designs they produced under the Folly Cove Designers' name to the public again, and they donated all their sample books, prints, and remnants to the Cape Ann Historical Association, where they remain to this day.

Also languishing in the museum archives are the beginnings of a book that Houghton Mifflin had hoped would exhibit Burton's expertise, teaching ability, and artistic sense of style in the world of design. Sometime in the early 1940s, adult trade book editor Paul Brooks suggested that Burton write a book incorporating her theories and practice. He was in agreement with Burton's strongly held belief that "others can learn to make their own design and apply it to any of the other crafts." A memo in the archives indicates that she signed a contract for the book—to be called *Design and How!*—on June 13, 1949.

Over the next fifteen years or so, Brooks encouraged, cajoled, and, in his words, "tried to browbeat" Burton into finishing the task. A letter of November 12, 1950, indicates that she hoped to have it finished by March 1, 1951, and mentions that she had told children's editor Jean Poindexter Colby not to expect *Maybelle the Cable Car* until *Design and How!* was done. In 1954, she wrote Brooks, "Your visit has inspired and spurred me on to get right to work on *Design and How*!!! Now I believe you really want the book and of course I really want to get it done . . . so I shall practice the first rule in the book and Do It." On May 11, 1961, Brooks wrote to Burton to ask if *Design and How!* would ever get delivered, saying, "To me this is roughly the equivalent of finding a live dodo in the frog pond." Again, on January 4, 1963, he gently prodded: "Can I persuade you that this is your duty, your pleasure and a future source of profit for both of us and our grandchildren?" On May 7, 1963, Brooks wrote a memo to a

Facing page: "Zaidee and Her Kittens" by Virginia Lee Demetrios (no date)

Barbara Cain at Houghton Mifflin, saying that he hoped that Burton would finish *Design and How!* for the 1964 or 1965 list. And indeed, in a 1964 article, when asked what she was working on, she replied, "I must get at the one on design." However, it never happened. Her increasingly poor health and her eight-year-long work on *Life Story* consumed her last years. Although her sons hoped years ago that the book could somehow be finished and published, and Mary Ann Lash still feels that it should be revived, others feel that time and changes in technique in the world of design have closed the door to such a possibility.

Many of the original members are deceased, and few today remember

the precision, care, and dedication of the small cadre of people called the Folly Cove Designers. One group is trying to change that: the Windhover Dancers on Cape Ann recently produced an innovative tribute to the former textile collective. Ina Hahn, a former Folly Cove Designer and a dance teacher of Burton's, has effectively combined dance, narration, and music to create *Once in Folly Cove*. Through this combination, Hahn has

Facing page: When success increased their reputation, this barn became home to the Folly Cove Designers' exhibitions. Locals and visitors purchased hundreds of place mats, skirts, aprons, and table runners, as well as fabrics by the yard. HOUGHTON MIFFLIN COMPANY ARCHIVES

"translated" the Folly Cove designs into rhythmic and fluid choreography that expresses the movement of the original work. The accompanying narration, written by Pat Earle, credits Burton and the others as being "giants of their time." Other than this performance, it is only in the annals of museums where the Folly Cove products have been exhibited and in books, pamphlets, and articles that describe their work that testimony to the Folly Cove Designers can still be found. Folly Cove was, Burton said, "not only a place but a state of mind."

Katy also had a snow plow
to plow snow with.

Katy, sporting a valentine-shaped snowplow, sits poised waiting to be called to duty; meanwhile, miniature Katys chug through the snow in a perfectly designed frame that neatly sets the scene. *KATY AND THE BIG SNOW*

6 KATY, ROBIN, AND MAYBELLE

REGARDLESS OF THE GROWING SUCCESS OF THE FOLLY COVE DESIGNERS and the Caldecott Medal on her mantel, Burton didn't rest long on her laurels. *Katy and the Big Snow* (1943), featuring the tractor with a heart-shaped snowplow, followed close behind. Once again, a close-to-home situation fueled the idea — and once again, Burton began her project with research and firsthand, on-site experiences.

"Katy," Burton said, "was the pride and joy of the Gloucester Highway Department." She took her son Aris with her into the machine cab so she could see its working parts. "I was more fascinated than he," she said about the incident. Aris laughingly remembers: "She was right, I was terrified." While she was working on *Katy,* a snowstorm blew into Boston, and, as her editor Lee Kingman Natti recalls, Burton rushed to the city to sketch scenes from Houghton Mifflin's office windows and to follow a snowblower, a new vehicle on the winter scene, around the streets. The new machine, however, never appeared in the book, as Burton was convinced that the old but trusty plow was a much better heroine. As in *Mike Mulligan* and *Choo Choo,* Burton found comfort in the endurance and reliability of the tried and true.

The setting for *Katy,* the city of Geoppolis, which Burton visually outlines complete with numbers keyed to the individual places drawn in the

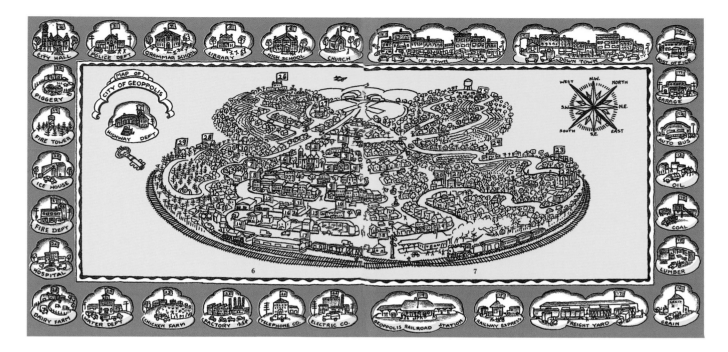

Burton's attention to detail comes to light in this pictorial map of Geoppolis, the scene of Katy's triumph over a tremendous blizzard. *KATY AND THE BIG SNOW*

margins, is in fact central Gloucester, only five miles from where Burton lived. The story revolves around Katy, the powerful tractor who "liked to work—the harder and tougher the job the better." When a blizzard hits Geoppolis, blocking the town from one end to the other, Katy, or K.T., as is emblazoned on her truck, is the only one strong enough to get through the snow. One by one, as she liberates the police, mail carriers, electric and telephone linemen, doctors, firefighters, airport runways, and city streets, a rhythm emerges in the words and in the pictures. In the end, Katy unifies the town, making it once more a bustling, working community. Although *Katy* might have benefited from a human being in the machine's cab or a bit more conflict to the plot, the story possesses a little-engine-that-could energy that, like a magnet, grabs children's emotions. Each year when winter rolls around, the book is again in demand.

It would be four years before Burton would publish her next book, *Song of Robin Hood,* which brought her a second Caldecott acclamation, this time an Honor Book citation. Although Roger Duvoisin's illustrations for Alvin Tresselt's *White Snow, Bright Snow,* which won the medal that year,

The dedication page for *Katy and the Big Snow*, which is a veritable history of Burton's work to date (1943), was adapted by Houghton Mifflin into a classy advertisement for the author's books. PUBLISHERS WEEKLY, JANUARY 19, 1943

BY *Virginia Lee Burton*

CALDECOTT AWARD
WINNER

Katy and the Big Snow $2.00

Watch for it — coming next fall

The Little House

CALDECOTT AWARD — 1942

$1.25

Calico
THE WONDER HORSE
or the Saga
of Stewy Slinker
$1.00

Mike Mulligan
and
his Steam Shovel
$1.75

Choo Choo
now $2.00

HOUGHTON MIFFLIN COMPANY · PUBLISHERS

undoubtedly received the higher merit for their child appeal, it is difficult to understand why Burton's artistry for *Song of Robin Hood* wouldn't have tipped the scale in her favor.

The 1950s were years filled with requests for speeches and autograph

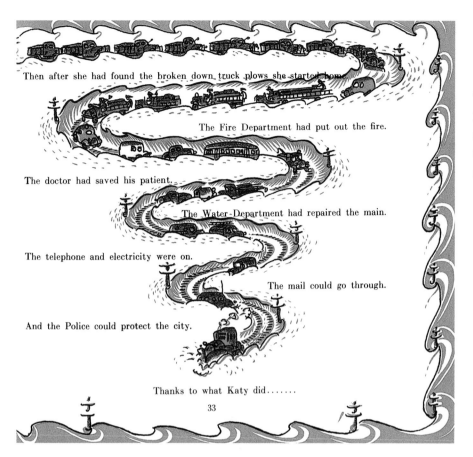

Then after she had found the broken down truck plows she started home.

The Fire Department had put out the fire.

The doctor had saved his patient.

The Water-Department had repaired the main.

The telephone and electricity were on.

The mail could go through.

And the Police could protect the city.

Thanks to what Katy did.......

33

This page from *Katy* exemplifies Burton's expert ability at integrating story and picture and then situating them smoothly into an overall design concept. *KATY AND THE BIG SNOW*

signings, but even in an era when children's authors and illustrators were less on stage than they are today, Burton participated only minimally. She may, in fact, have deliberately played down her rising fame, as her steadily growing income was a source of tension between her and her husband. In son Michael's words, "My father was a patriarchal Greek male who felt keenly about his wife being the breadwinner. They had terrible fights, and we (Aris and I) were often caught in the middle." He hastens to say that his parents never lost their mutual respect and admiration for each other's artistic abilities and that each found in the other a touchstone for creative energy. And, he says, their passion for their home and lifestyle united them.

At Christmas, for instance, Virginia made her own Christmas cards and delighted in baking special foods. For Christmas Eve, she transformed her barn studio, draping green boughs tied with red ribbons around the walls

Christmas was a joyous time in the Demetrios household, and each year Virginia created a beautiful, intricately designed greeting card to send to family and friends. COURTESY OF THE DEMETRIOS FAMILY

and hanging up Christmas cards, especially those handmade by artist friends. After Aris and Michael grew up and moved to California, they sent home bright red paper ornaments from San Francisco's Chinatown to further brighten the festivities. Friends and neighbors were invited for a Christmas Eve carol-singing party, where a buffet of ham, cheese, homemade Greek bread, and plenty of wine and beer awaited. Virginia played her small spinet, which was wheeled into the middle of the room, and the high point of the evening was the singing of "The Twelve Days of Christmas," with first a soloist, then a duo, then a trio, and eventually everyone joining in.

Unfortunately, Burton never illustrated this old ballad. The first half of

Facing page: Virginia, exquisitely dressed, plays the spinet for a Christmas Eve celebration. GERDA PETERICH, 1960, COURTESY OF THE DEMETRIOS FAMILY

the 1940s, however, found her concentrating on a series of ballads; the resulting book's preparation and production is a story in itself.

Song of Robin Hood can surely be called Burton's artistic tour de force. The genesis for the book began in 1941. Back when Burton was engrossed in illustrations for *The Little House,* then children's editor Grace Hogarth contracted with anthologist Anne Malcolmson to produce a book about Robin Hood. Malcolmson scoured old songbooks and found original music for fifteen old airs about the legendary champion of Sherwood Forest. Three more ballads, without music, were included, for a total of eighteen. After engaging Grace Castagnetta to set the melodies in modern notation, Hogarth asked Burton to be the artist because, according to Natti, the subject "craved the bold liveliness of her illustration."

It was surely a labor of love. Burton devoted two years to developing a medium and technique suitable for the project. All that stopped her work was the ripening of the abundant vegetable garden to canning status. While their father was helpful, son Michael recalls, "my brother and I became what we thought at the time was forced labor—working the garden, tending the goats, and harvesting the crops." During the winter Burton huddled over her drawing board, wearing fur-lined boots to keep her feet warm and keeping a mug of coffee within reach on top of a small coal-burning stove. It was their father rather than their mother who was the disciplinarian, according to Aris. "He was very strict and tried to make meals into lecture sessions about artistic principles until my mother would intervene, telling him to 'lighten up,' which sometimes began one of their royal battles. I guess he worried that we would not be exposed to enough culture because of the remote area where we lived."

The rendering of the illustrations for *Song of Robin Hood* once again

ROBIN HOOD AND THE GOLDEN ARROW

Burton's sons are here, in disguise; they donned costumes, learned to handle bows and arrows, and struck poses as their mother sketched pictures to get the right angle and appropriate stance.
THE SONG OF ROBIN HOOD, EDITED BY ANNE MALCOLMSON

involved her family. To ensure authenticity, Burton studied tapestries and parchments and borrowed a twelfth-century sword to guide her drawings. After buying tights and making jerkins, she rallied her nephew Costa and her sons to be her models. Burton commented, "With the whole family taking up archery, Folly Cove became Sherwood Forest and I could draw my subjects from life." Perhaps that is why in the lower right-hand corner of the page of plant listings one finds tiny print decreeing "To Aris and Mike from Mummy." In those days, only the author

Burton's interest in design comes to the forefront in her work for *Song of Robin Hood*, seen here in her use of black, gray, and white; the graduated patterns of the plants and trees; and the sense of perspective she brings to the page.

had the privilege of dedication; Burton, however, found a clever way to secrete one into a scroll.

Careful inspection of *Song of Robin Hood* gives viewers a clear understanding of Burton's design philosophy, in which she effectively employed blacks, grays, and whites in imaginative ways. Her study of twelfth-century English illuminated manuscripts, which monks scribed by hand, inspired Burton to illustrate the more than four hundred verses in keeping with the spirit of that earlier time. Although this added a whole year to the preparation of the book, she justified the effort by saying that it resulted in a better balance in the proportion of text to picture on each page and, more important, brought out the action of the ballads.

The medieval monks, Burton had discovered, had embellished their work with familiar flowers and vines. Her own joy in nature found this a natural link, and she searched for plants that had grown in twelfth-century England, some of which she found in her own backyard. In the introduction, Burton credits help from *The Observer's Book of British Wild Flowers,* sent to her by an American serviceman stationed in England, and *The History of the Vegetable Kingdom,* lent to her by a friend.

In addition to a list of these plants and the reason they were chosen, Burton supplied an extensive explanation about her choices. Her words combine with Malcolmson's author's note and a seven-page glossary to give a rich background to this highly imaginative, creative effort.

The story behind *Song of Robin Hood* doesn't end, however, with Burton's four-year toil over the illustrations. Jean Poindexter Colby, production manager at Houghton Mifflin in those years, continues the story. When each of the 128 pages of art, which Burton did in a combination of pen-and-ink and scratchboard, was completed, the original drawings were hand-carried (to ensure delivery) to the engravers to make the plates. These were then delivered, again by hand, to the Riverside Press, where the task of combining text and picture began. The precision necessary to reproduce the delicate images, the work to balance the effect that Burton was trying to create, and the difficulty of finding high-quality paper and printing inks (a problem in the immediate postwar years) added months to production. Trouble stalked Colby and Burton at every turn. At one point, because of drying problems, ten thousand sheets had to be

Facing page: Noteworthy here is the illustrator's use of intertwining tendrils that weave around the first letter of each verse. For each ballad Burton selected different and appropriate flora —she chose the wild rose and weeping willow as suitable for this one. SONG OF ROBIN HOOD

And Marian, poor soul, was troubled in mind
  For the absence of her friend.
With finger to eye, she'd often cry
  And his person much commend.

Perplexed and vexed and troubled in mind,
  She dressed herself like a page,
And searched the wood for Robin Hood,
  The bravest of men in that age.

With quiver and bow, sword, buckler, and all,
  Thus armed was Marian most bold,
Still wandering about to find Robin out,
  Whose presence was better than gold.

But Robin Hood himself disguised,
  And Marian was strangely attired.
So they proved foes, and fell to blows.
  Her valor bold Robin admired.

They drew their swords and to cutting they went,
  For at least an hour or more,
Till blood ran apace from Robin's face,
  And Marian was wounded sore.

reprinted. Both Burton and Colby went on press, and, Colby reports, "We became such common visitors to the pressroom that one of the men asked if we had joined the union."

The cover design provided another challenge; Burton's chain-mail design needed to be printed rather than stamped, and the initial effect, Colby said, was "simply awful." Eventually, with the help of several knowledgeable pressmen at Riverside, an outside lithographer, and Burton herself, a solution was reached. By putting the title and an image of Robin Hood's horn in silver against a black background, bordering it in bright red, and placing it near the top left corner against the chain-mail pattern, they obtained the precise look they wanted. The renowned Bertha Mahony Miller of *The Horn Book Magazine* called the book one of "special skill and distinction," saying, "it is such amazingly fine and beautiful work that it should be brought to the attention of the public constantly." Houghton Mifflin has done just that. *Song of Robin Hood,* which had been unavailable for years, was brought back into print in 2000. None of the painstaking fifty-three-year-old work has been lost; it is still a book of "special skill and distinction."

As Burton's children grew older and she no longer had their life experiences to call on, Burton looked to a favorite tale from her own childhood, Hans Christian Andersen's *The Emperor's New Clothes.* She remembered her father reading it to her when she was a child. Her dedication reads, "With appreciation to my Father who shared his enjoyment of this story with his children," and pictures a man reading to three children — undoubtedly Burton and her two siblings. Archives hold ten versions of this dedication page — a fascinating example of how she arranged and rearranged image and text in order to get the balance, harmony, and design she wanted.

Fanciful colors and decorations bring this well-loved Andersen tale to a jovial conclusion. *THE EMPEROR'S NEW CLOTHES* BY HANS CHRISTIAN ANDERSEN

The Emperor felt very silly
for he knew that the people were right
but he thought, "The procession has started
and it must go on now!"

So the Lords of the Bedchamber
held their heads higher than ever
and took greater trouble to pretend
to hold up the train which wasn't there at all.

THE END

In fashioning the multicharacter scenes for *The Emperor's New Clothes*, Burton drew on one of her husband's mandates — "Learn to see a figure in its entirety and put it on the paper rapidly." An array of characters, dressed in seventeenth-century opulence, populates the pages. She portrayed them not so much as individuals but as members of a Greek chorus who bolster and support the telling. While adding to the overall visual structure, each character still has a vitality of his or her own. In much the same way, her anthropomorphized houses become secondary characters,

No hill too steep . . .
no load too heavy . . .
Always cheerful . . .
and most polite . . .

She rang her gong
and sang her song
from early morn
till late at night.

Lampposts stud the page, giving ballast to Maybelle and providing a guide for the reader as the cable car streams along. *MAYBELLE THE CABLE CAR*

and her humming looms quicken the action. The Emperor's parade, a seemingly endless procession, drives the story's humor and inspires inspection right to the corner of each page. The book was a return to color for Burton, and her bright — just short of garish — and varied hues emphasize both the elegance and the silliness of the Emperor.

Concerned as always about the balance between text and image, she retold the story in her own words. An anomaly to Andersen purists, the retelling nevertheless allowed her to give visual structure to the words, which she could then manipulate into her overall design.

By the 1950s, Burton, who had reconciled with her mother, was making cross-country trips to California. Possibly one of these visits — or her memories of commuting to the city — inspired her to create *Maybelle the Cable Car.* Published in 1952, the book was a tribute to a city she loved.

In a tussle between buses and cable cars, the arrogant Big Bill suddenly finds the hills of San Francisco a challenge; once again, Burton pits the new against the old. *MAYBELLE THE CABLE CAR*

Then came one damp and foggy night
when Big Bill tried to stop half way down.
He slipped . . . he slid . . . he turned around.
"Whew, that was close," groaned Bill.
"I don't think I like this hill."

In her own words, Burton was motivated to provide a visual "history of the cable car and how the people of San Francisco prevented its demise." In *Maybelle,* she returned to several themes used in *Mike Mulligan, The Little House,* and *Choo Choo*—survival through determination, a delight in old-fashioned spunk, and the celebration of the tried and true.

The action revolves around Maybelle's possible displacement by city buses. However, when arrogant Big Bill can't negotiate San Francisco's precipitous streets and the community sides with Maybelle, the cable cars triumph. Perhaps too full of information about the workings of the cable car and the details of an election to be called a story, and too fictional to rate as an information book today, *Maybelle* nevertheless beguiles many travelers and ends up in their suitcases after a visit to the City by the Bay.

What propels many of Burton's titles, this one included, is the authen-

ticity of her research. Asked what she liked best about creating juvenile books, Burton answered, "Research mainly. I love research because I have so much fun doing it. By the time I was satisfied with my sketches [for *Maybelle*], I could operate a cable car." She once remarked, "Children have an avid appetite for knowledge. They like to learn, provided that the subject matter is presented to them in an entertaining way."

Her portrayals of familiar San Francisco landmarks — the Golden Gate

Facing page: On a visit to San Francisco to present her artwork to the San Francisco Public Library, Burton posed at the cable car's turnaround spot with one of the long-time drivers. HOUGHTON MIFFLIN COMPANY ARCHIVES

Bridge, City Hall, the Ferry Building, and the steep streets — make *Maybelle* a nostalgia lover's dream. The book, however, also demonstrates the voice of democracy at work, and many a teacher has used it in the classroom as an example of "making a difference." With a plucky protagonist at the helm and a text full of "Ting, Tings," "Dong Dings," and "HoooOOOLD ONs," the story rings with Burton's characteristic energy.

Maybelle was dedicated to Mrs. Hans Klussman, who, Burton said, was "a leading light in the fight to save [cable cars] from extinction." The book itself has been credited with helping to preserve the famous cars. At a ceremony on December 10, 1967, Burton made a gift of the original manuscript and illustrations to the San Francisco Public Library, including some preliminary sketches that were never used. She attended the ceremony with her grandson and was presented with a miniature silver replica of a cable car.

PHOTOGRAPH BY GERDA PETERICH, 1960, COURTESY OF THE DEMETRIOS FAMILY

7 THE WANING YEARS

AFTER THE PUBLICATION OF *MAYBELLE* IN 1952, FANS OF BURTON WOULD wait ten years for the next book by the esteemed author. The book, *Life Story*, would take her eight years to research, write, and illustrate. Meanwhile, her life in Folly Cove changed little. A 1964 article in the Gloucester paper quoted George Demetrios: "I work every day — all day. But I love it. I have never known a day off. Why would I want one when there are so many wonderful things to do in the world? I find my relaxation in variety, in doing different things — sculpturing, drawing, teaching, writing, gardening, grass cutting, sheep feeding."

Like her husband, Burton was strongly influenced by her physical environment and by the ever-changing aspects of nature. According to Lee Kingman Natti, it seemed natural that Burton would one day revisit the theme of *The Little House*. In *Life Story*, Burton did just that; but she broadened the scene, putting it into the context of the history of the world.

After telling the story of life on Earth from its earliest beginnings, two million years ago, to the present day, Burton takes readers to Folly Cove, letting them embrace the world she lived in for twenty-five years. The final pages hold a very personal account of her family, pets, gardens, and home. One can see the driveway curving up from the road, the house and studio, a small shed for their sheep, George's woodpiles, and the field of daisies Jinnee so loved, which she had pictured extensively in *The Little House*. The images are full of activity from real life: George mowing the lawn, the boys shoveling snow, Costa gathering apples, a baby playing in the shade of the swing tree, and Burton herself painting on the sidelines. And while she drew the house she lived in more realistically than the idealized cottage she portrayed in *The Little House,* that pink-roofed Cape Cod cottage still shows up opposite the title page.

Much of her research for *Life Story*—studying hundreds of works on geology, paleontology, paleobotany, and archaeology—took place at the American Museum of Natural History in New York. At times Burton stayed in a nearby hotel to be closer to the facility, saying at one point, "I can tell you, the employees of the Museum got very weary seeing me parked on their front steps morning after morning." The painstaking study and full-color originals exhausted her physically and creatively, editor Natti recalls, but Burton's patience with the infinite details and determination to "get it right" drove her in the eight-year task. Perfection was her continual goal—she had little time for illustrators whose work was too quick, unfinished, or imitative.

Bertha Mahony Miller wrote to Burton after receiving *Life Story,* "It seems to me that work like yours which produces each book different from all the others and which spares no time or pains to bring a vision to fulfillment deserves very special recognition. The book is so grand that all I can say is—I take off my shoes before you!"

Life Story was critically acclaimed, and a festive party was held at Boston's Museum of Science. The book found its way to New York's Fifth

Facing page: The gardens and orchards of Burton's home, seen here in a spread from *Life Story*, yielded food for the table. A visitor commented in the *Christian Science Monitor* (January 25, 1944) that the cellar was filled with "row upon colorful row, shelf after shelf—more than 500 cans—of vegetables, fruits, meats, jams, jellies, conserves, and pickles. She managed to do all of this and she also met publishers' deadlines."

Avenue, where sketches, original drawings, and copies of the book dressed department store windows.

Burton executed the seventy-two-page book, with its thirty-five full-color illustrations, in an inventive way that harked back to her love of theater: the story plays out on a stage with a proscenium arch, in a prologue, five acts, and an epilogue. The passing of time is depicted by clocks, cal-

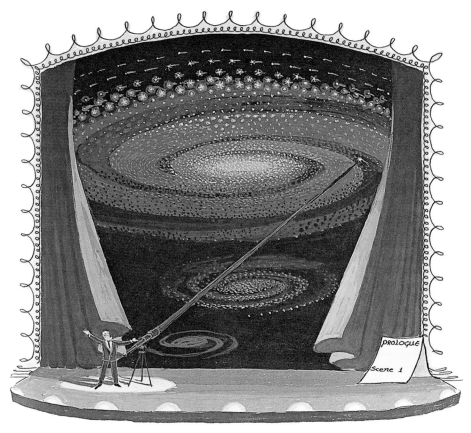

The astronomer in this prologue gives way to a geologist in Act I (Paleozoic Era), a paleontologist in Act II (Mesozoic Era), a historian in Act III (Cenozoic Era), a grandmother in Act IV (Recent Life), and Burton herself in Act V, who introduces readers to her life and home in Folly Cove. *LIFE STORY*

endars, shadows, and, in the early "chapters," the appearance and disappearance of animals.

The Prologue, scene 1, features an astronomer at stage right, where pulled-back curtains reveal a whirling galaxy of stars. The right-hand side of the page amplifies the scene, depicting various galaxies, including Earth's, with accompanying text.

Continuing this format, the next five scenes introduce the sun, the earth, the moon, and various rocks. Then, in the Epilogue, Burton speaks directly to her audience: "It is now your Life Story and it is you who play the leading role. . . . The drama of Life is a continuous story — ever new, ever changing, and ever wondrous to behold." She cleverly presents the story of life on Earth as a wondrous drama and succeeds in giving readers a sense of their own place in the flow of time and cre-

Archives provide evidence of Burton's strive for perfection; this scene in *Life Story*, for example, was repainted numerous times, each with a slightly different emphasis or viewpoint, until she was satisfied.

ation as well as a sense of belonging to the continuously evolving world in which they live.

Burton repeats a major theme of her books, and a precept that she found necessary in her own personal life story — survival through change. In Act I she writes, "Life in order to survive was forced to adapt or to change." She believed in the continuity of life — as evidenced in the Little House's return to the country, in Mary Anne's newfound job, in Maybelle's continuing negotiation of San Francisco's hills. In *Life Story* she brings that belief to the forefront for readers to ponder.

The design concept is very effective. The front endpapers are black, signifying the emptiness of the universe at the beginning, while the bright yellow back endpapers emphasize tomorrow's promise. Evolutionary changes, embedded in her signature spiral designs, appear in

many of the scenes. At the time of publication, Harvard geology professor Kirtley F. Mather noted, "Miss Burton is to be congratulated upon
her success in presenting so many important items of historical Geology
without underestimating the intelligence and scientific curiosity of her
prospective audience."

Facing page: For *Life Story*, Burton created thirty-five full-color paintings and accompanying line drawings that reveal the changing face of Earth — here, the Ice Age — demonstrating that all the world is truly a stage. The project took her eight years.

Life Story, The Little House, Katy and the Big Snow, and *Choo Choo* have been translated into Japanese, and in fact *The Little House,* according to a *Gloucester Daily Times* article, was considered a pioneer work in such translation. The popularity of her books in Japan motivated the American Cultural Center in Tokyo to invite Burton to speak and autograph copies of her books in 1964. During her two-week trip she met and became friends with Kyoko Matsuko, who took Burton to the far reaches of the country and introduced her to people who had long admired her books. She said that spending four days near Mt. Fuji in a fishing village was "like living in a Japanese print." At Burton's departure she was given samurai swords from the seventeenth and eighteenth centuries as tokens of appreciation. Greatly impressed with her experiences, Burton talked of creating a book with a Japanese background, but only a sketchbook of drawings from her visit remains.

While she continued to work on and improve *Design and How!,* the book was never finished. Burton talked about other book possibilities for young readers, but they never happened. She thought about a book concerned with building a house, and planned to accompany the text with large illustrations and diagrams showing the fine points of structure and carpentry. The Burton files at the Cape Ann Historical Association include blueprints of the house she lived in and the additions made after the 1947 fire; perhaps these floor plans would have been research tools had her idea come to fruition.

A rough dummy and a few sketches indicate thoughts of writing a book called *Lefty, the Bird Dog* or *Kippy. Lefty,* her Newfoundland dog that followed her everywhere — often to the cove where she swam, and where he chased seagulls — would probably have been the model. However, a prophetic comment in Burton's handwriting, "No plot, no story," reveals its destiny. Perhaps she could not see Lefty as a protagonist, or perhaps her worsening health had sapped her creativity, but another book was never completed.

In Burton's last years, cancer took over her body. The affront was not only physical but also emotional: her strong New England conscience thought any kind of illness a sign of weakness. She filled her last days with walks through the woods, often bringing home budded twigs, flowers, and grasses, which she would sketch and paint. A huge rock that juts into the sea near Burton's home was a favorite place for her to lie in the sun and be near the water. It became known as Jinnee's Rock. She bought a Mustang convertible (which didn't raise her spirits as she hoped), decorated a small hallway of her home in a rose motif, and painted designs on high chairs and toy boxes for her grandchildren. Burton also spent several years creating a four-paneled reversible screen that shows the details

Facing page: The Four Seasons by Virginia Lee Burton Demetrios. Oil on wood panels, late 1950s

Dancers by Virginia Lee Burton Demetrios. Wood carving, late 1930s

of a nearby brook, across the seasons. This piece, like one she created during a summer in Fiesole, Italy, with her husband, has been said to be of museum quality.

Virginia Lee Burton died on October 15, 1968. Devastated by her death, George found refuge in his work. He cast a nearly life-size bronze statue of Jinnee—her arms flung skyward, her head back, one leg kicked high—personifying her love of dance and love of life. At Virginia's request, her ashes were spread in the acreage around their home—the place that had nurtured her personal life and creative efforts for so many years.

Jinnee Goes to Heaven by George Demetrios. Bronze, circa 1969

COURTESY OF THE DEMETRIOS FAMILY

8 THE LEGEND LIVES ON

BURTON'S PEN MAY HAVE BEEN STILLED AND THE FOLLY COVE DESIGNS packed away, but her stories spin on across time. Mike Mulligan, Katy, Maybelle, Choo Choo, and the Little House have, over the years, slipped into the American culture — but probably none so much as *Mike Mulligan and His Steam Shovel.*

An early indication of this title's immortality appeared in 1954, when Burton was still alive. Author Julia Sauer, head of the Rochester (New York) Public Library, who undoubtedly witnessed Burton's popularity on a day-to-day basis with the children she served, wrote *Mike's House,* a book about a boy who, when lost, tells a friendly policeman that he needs to get to "Mike's house" — which turns out to be the local library that houses his favorite book, *Mike Mulligan and His Steam Shovel.* Brought to life by Don Freeman's illustrations, the book was an early salute to *Mike Mulligan*'s popularity with children — a popularity that endures to this day.

Beverly Cleary is another author to give a nod to *Mike Mulligan.* In *Ramona the Pest,* published in 1968 (the year of Burton's death), Ramona's teacher, Miss Binney, reads aloud *Mike Mulligan and His Steam Shovel.* The story is a favorite of Ramona's because "unlike so many books for her age, it was neither quiet and sleepy nor sweet and pretty."

Mike Mulligan has become known far beyond the children's literature community as well. In an article in *The Horn Book Newsletter,* author Amy Cohn tells of her lifelong love affair with Mike and Mary Anne and mentions a structural engineer's claim that *Mike Mulligan* inspired his career choice, calling the book a "romance about the love of a man for a beguiling heroine dramatically trapped in life-threatening circumstances." Jim Trelease, children's literature advocate and lecturer, relates a story about a college student who could still recite *Mike Mulligan* word for word years after hearing it as a child.

Burton's son Mike recounts how he and his college roommate once began discussing favorite childhood books. Knowing his friend only as Michael Demetrios, the roommate suddenly said, "My all-time favorite book as a child was *Mike Mulligan and His Steam Shovel.*" The roommate's face flashed with total surprise when Michael announced, "I'm Mike."

"How do you get to Popperville? We want to go to Popperville to see Mike Mulligan," wrote a young boy from Philadelphia in a letter to Burton in 1972. Long after her death, Houghton Mifflin still receives correspondence asking about Burton, requesting her autograph, or containing children's drawings of favorite Burton characters. In 1982, someone even submitted a sequel to *Mike Mulligan*—called "Mary Anne to the Rescue"—to Houghton Mifflin's editorial department; it was gently but firmly turned down.

Before Christmas in 1999, the chain store Restoration Hardware ordered thousands of copies of *Mike Mulligan* for its stores nationwide and quickly sold them all to adults who remembered the trusty steam shovel from their childhood. In some cases, they now wanted to share the book with their grandchildren; others simply bought the book for their own enjoyment.

Facing page: Burton fascinated children with her stories; attraction still holds today when young readers meet the likes of Mike and Mary Anne, the Little House, Maybelle, Katy, and Choo Choo. CAPE ANN HISTORICAL ASSOCIATION

In Jay Leno's *Leading with My Chin,* the comedian wonders why he turned out the way he did, and makes the point that one can't be funny by oneself. "There is one line in *Mike Mulligan and His Steam Shovel* that sums up my life. When Mike and his old steam shovel Mary Anne are digging a hole for a skyscraper, a line reads, 'When people used to stop and

Facing page: A toy model of Mary Anne, produced by Schylling, Inc.

watch them, Mike Mulligan and Mary Anne used to dig a little faster and a little better. The more people stopped, the faster and the better they dug.' And that made sense to me, a perfectly logical reason to dig a great hole or act like an idiot in public." Although the hole Mike and Mary Anne dug was for a small village town hall, not a skyscraper, the impact on Leno is noteworthy.

This same message comes out in the article "Books That Last" for *Five Owls*. Critic Norine Odland discusses *Mike Mulligan* in light of the theme that work is best accomplished together through mutual respect and admiration. She comments that "children often repeat Burton's lines 'we always work faster and better when someone is watching us' — without necessarily remembering where they came from."

In a *Newsweek* essay, "Goodbye, Mike Mulligan," writer Robert J. Samuelson, writing about the inevitability of change, uses *Mike Mulligan* as a touchstone, remarking that Burton "had a genius for reducing these epic upheavals to small sagas of the human spirit." *Time* magazine writer Robert Wright also calls on *Mike Mulligan* in "The Mike Mulligan Moment," an article about the impact of technology.

In an article entitled "The End of Innocence," *New York Times* critic A. O. Scott, writing about the Harry Potter phenomenon, talks about books of lasting value over the years. He cites *Mike Mulligan* as an example of a title that sits comfortably alongside such contemporary books as Jon Scieszka and Lane Smith's *The Stinky Cheese Man* and Janell Cannon's *Stellaluna*.

Mike Mulligan is also a longtime favorite with homeschoolers. On the message boards of the Web site "Five in a Row," parent-teachers enthusiastically describe using *Mike Mulligan* in studies about personification and onomatopoeia, road construction, earth movers, simple machines, and steam power, and they discuss other Burton books as well, exploring her work as author and illustrator.

Mike also surfaces in the fine arts. *Mike Mulligan and His Steam Shovel* has been adapted and performed by various children's theater groups across the country. It was successfully staged by the Lifeline Theater in Chicago (1998) and by Milwaukee's FirstStage Children's Theater (2002) with original music by Eric Lanes Barnes, and in 2000 Stephen Simon wrote his own musical version, narrated by television actor Gavin MacLeod, for a performance by the Cape Symphony Orchestra in Barnstable, Massachusetts.

Children relate to Mary Anne in a very personal way. Phyllis Fenner, in *The Proof of the Pudding,* tells this story: A woman, driving her grandchildren along a road one day, hears them suddenly shriek, "Stop, there's Mary Anne." Believing it to be a friend of the children, she slams on her brakes, only to discover that the object of their attention is a machine digging in a construction site!

Just as *Mike Mulligan* led Boston children in a grand celebration for its sixtieth anniversary, in 2002 *The Little House* will enjoy an anniversary of its own. Sixty years after it was published, and nearly thirty-five years after Burton's death, the book is another of those rare titles that continues to be enjoyed by children and acclaimed by adults. Like many of Burton's books, it too has taken on a life of its own.

The *National Observer* ran a news story in 1967 telling how an eighteenth-century farmhouse situated "amid towering concrete and masonry" was moved from East 71st Street and York in Manhattan to a new life on Charles Street in Greenwich Village. Alongside the photo of the house being relocated, the editor included an image of a similar scene from *The Little House.*

Facing page: The power of association brought *The Little House* into the news in 1967. PHOTOGRAPH FROM UPI. *NATIONAL OBSERVER*, MARCH 13, 1967

The Little House

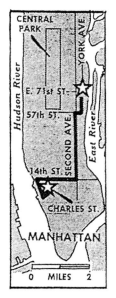

In life, the little house at Second Avenue and 42nd.

In fiction, the little house amid skyscrapers.

Photograph from UPI; Drawing Courtesy Houghton Mifflin Co.

"THEY went to the Movers to see if the Little House could be moved. The Movers looked the Little House all over and said, 'Sure, this house is as good as ever. She's built so well we could move her anywhere.' So they jacked up the Little House and put her on wheels."

The words are from Virginia Lee Burton's 'The Little House,' published in 1942. Still a popular book, it tells of a farmhouse that is almost elbowed into oblivion by the city before it is moved to a new location and becomes a home once more. Last week the story and this drawing of 'The Little House' came to life in New York City. An Eighteenth Century farmhouse, situated amid towering concrete and masonry at York Avenue and East 71st in Manhattan, was placed on a flatbed trailer and moved five miles past skyscrapers to a new life as a private home on Charles Street in Greenwich Village.

The move cost Mr. and Mrs. Sven Bernhard, the owners, $1,500 a mile. The two-story frame house had to be moved to make way for a home for the aged.

A 1986 *New York Times* article by author Anne Tyler describes her life-long fascination with Burton's Caldecott winner. "I have returned to *The Little House* over and over, sinking into its colorful, complicated pictures all through childhood and adolescence and adulthood. First my parents read it to me, then I read it to myself. I believe the book spoke to me about something I hadn't yet consciously considered: the passage of time. And it introduced me to the feeling of nostalgia — the realization of the losses that the passage of time can bring."

In an article in *Historic Preservation* magazine, Charles Clark, a parent and ardent conservationist, asserts: "Whether you belong to the posse that's intent on fending barbarians off the heritage, or whether you acquire a taste for the wrecking ball, depends on whether you grow up with the books of Virginia Lee Burton." He calls her books "an underused secret weapon in the preservationist arsenal" and suggests sending the next child born in the neighborhood not an Erector set but a copy of *The Little House*.

Burton might well be credited with paving the way for a much loved and popular theme in children's books: a specific place as a measure of the passing of time. But it isn't only Burton's themes that surface in other children's books. The plots and characters she concocted echo in such titles as Bill Peet's *Smokey*, Hardie Gramatky's *Little Toot*, and William Pène du Bois's *Flying Locomotive* — which ring, as Burton's books do, with the action, energy, and solid happy endings that children love.

Design influences on Burton can also be traced to other books published at the time. Wanda Gag's *Millions of Cats* and Boris Artzybasheff's *Seven Simeons*, for example, suggest a similar mind-set: the design of the page is integral to the entire concept of the book.

In the summer of 2000, *A Common Reader*, a mail-order book catalog, instituted a children's books section called "The Company of Books." Burton's *Life Story*, published thirty-eight years earlier, was one of their opening choices, hailed as "a bravura performance from a leading lady of children's literature."

In *American Picturebooks,* author Barbara Bader chose but five author-illustrators to discuss in a chapter entitled "The Storytellers." Of Burton, the only woman she included, Bader writes: "Burton knew exactly what she wanted in a picturebook, hers or another's, and she wanted a good deal—information and significant detail as well as the accustomed clarity, humor and imagination. The wonder is that she achieved what she wanted without losing the spontaneity that Ranlett, among many, praises in her work."

To view and study originals of Burton's works means hopscotching across the country, as they are housed at the University of Oregon (*Mike Mulligan and His Steam Shovel, Calico the Wonder Horse, Choo Choo, The Emperor's New Clothes,* and *The Fast Sooner Hound*), the San Francisco Public Library (*Maybelle the Cable Car*), the Kerlan Collection at the University of Minnesota (*The Little House*), the Free Library of Philadelphia (*Life Story*), the Boston Public Library (*Song of Robin Hood*), the Cape Ann Historical Association in Gloucester (Folly Cove designs and drafts from Burton's various works), and the Sawyer Public Library in Gloucester (*Katy and the Big Snow*). While it is unfortunate for the Burton devotee that the locations of these originals are so widespread, this dispersion does parallel Burton's concern about setting: most of her books are very place-oriented, and that she would want them to be stored where they "lived" seems a natural extension of her beliefs.

Son Aris calls Jinnee a paradigm of today's modern woman: raising two wild (in his words) sons, married to a macho husband, and carrying on a two-part career—all of this in the late 1930s and early 1940s, when life didn't contain many of today's time-saving technologies and few women had careers. She was, in his words, "simply amazing."

Burton's oeuvre was small—she wrote and illustrated only seven books and illustrated just six more, yet she continues to be recognized as one of the major American children's author-illustrators of the twentieth century. Her philosophy still strikes a chord with readers in the twenty-first century, and her fluid design, care with detail, and sense of story in text and image still reach out today to children, who live in a world quite different from the one in which she created her books.

Nevertheless, when the page opens to a small pink-roofed house in a meadow, a sturdy steam shovel challenged by a day's work, a snowplow called to duty, a cable car ready to take on the steepest street, a legendary archer prepared to do battle, or a stage disclosing the secrets of the world, children still wait in breathless wonder for the story to unfold. Virginia Lee Burton would be pleased.

Facing page: Virginia Lee by George Demetrios. Bronze, 1936. COURTESY OF THE DEMETRIOS FAMILY

Research, vital to the writing of biography, leads down many roads. Some are full of frustration and disappointment; others brim with surprise and satisfaction. While tracing the life of Virginia Lee Burton, I traveled all these roads in the course of my search.

Frustration, for example, came when I couldn't discover with whom Virginia Burton lived in Sonora, California, after her mother left the family, or what her feelings were about the situation. Neither was I able to ascertain how and when she and her mother reconciled.

Disappointment resulted from failure to receive answers to letters sent to the high school and the art school she attended in California. Nor was I able to verify reported information about her dance contract in New York.

Pleasant surprises, however, balanced these downturns. I learned, for instance, the history behind the "Dickie Birkenbush" footnote in *Mike Mulligan and His Steam Shovel,* which I had puzzled over for years. Mr. Berkenbush invited me to his home, and I even sat at the table where, as a boy, he listened to Burton tell his grandmother about her dilemma with the story she was writing. To be in the spot where he supplied the answer of what to do with Mary Anne was, indeed, a pleasure. After that, seeing an early manuscript of *Mike Mulligan* with Burton's handwritten note at the

From the 1965 *Horn Book* calendar, showing February (*above*) and April (*below*). COURTESY OF THE HORN BOOK, INC.

bottom, "Acknowledgments to Dickie Birkenbush," made the story come alive.

Several puzzles awaited me and several surprises were in store as I worked to establish a complete bibliography of Burton's work. A book by Kenneth Henderson, *The Manual of American Mountaineering* (American Alpine Club), listed in the Gale Literary Biography series as containing illustrations by Burton, was difficult to locate. Through the Internet I found a copy of a similar title by Henderson, *Handbook of American Mountaineering,* published by Houghton Mifflin and the American Alpine Club. While the included drawings were duplicates of those in the earlier book, neither her name nor that of any other illustrator was listed. Continual searching took me to the National Library Catalog, where I discovered that several editions of Henderson's book had been published. Eventually, I located the American Alpine Club's 1941 edition. Virtually a book of illustrations, which *are* credited to Burton, it opens with a brief introduction by Henderson. He explains that the text-only edition was rushed into publication for World War II defense needs and that the illustrations were now being printed as a companion volume. An unusual situation to say the least. Why her name is not on the Houghton Mifflin edition remains a mystery.

According *to Fiction, Folklore, Fantasy & Poetry for*

Children, 1876–1985, Burton provided illustrations for Ethel Calvert Phillips's *Belinda and the Singing Clock.* This information came as a surprise, as I hadn't found the book listed in any other bibliography. At first, Houghton Mifflin personnel were mystified as well, but eventually an archive copy was located at the Boston Public Library. Being able to add *Belinda* and *Manual of American Mountaineering* to Burton's bibliography is a great satisfaction.

Visiting places associated with the person under investigation illuminates one's research. I traveled to Folly Cove, where Burton lived much of her life, and experienced the sparkling bay waters and bracing sea winds that she appreciated and used so liberally in her Folly Cove design work. I visited the house and browsed in Burton's studio. Before the properties were sold, I helped her sons sort and clean out the books, papers, and manuscripts she had accumulated over her lifetime. An unexpected reward surfaced — the original sketch that Burton had used to fashion Slumber, the main character in *Sad-Faced Boy.* Serendipitously, I had earlier discovered a piece Burton had written about illustrating Bontemps' book; finding this drawing literally completed the picture. Another item to emerge was a soiled and dog-eared copy of *Fairies and Friendly Folk,* a songbook that Burton had illustrated — even her sons had been unaware of its existence.

These images show June (*above*) and November (*below*) from the 1965 *Horn Book* calendar. COURTESY OF THE HORN BOOK, INC.

Pleasure derived from delving into the archives at the University of Oregon; the Boston, Philadelphia, and Gloucester public libraries; and the Cape Ann Historical Association in Gloucester, Massachusetts. At Cape Ann I found dozens of Burton's sketchbooks, full of the doodles and visual thoughts that she had put on paper so many years before. Included were notes in preparation for her 1943 Caldecott speech; sketches of friends, family, and pets; and ideas for possible new books. In browsing through the pages, I felt I was being given a rare glimpse, though much too brief, into Burton's invigorating and astute artistic vision.

Research can be painstaking and dull; it can also be exciting and gratifying. As Burton said herself, "I love research because I have so much fun doing it." Research fascinates, perhaps, because it leads down many tantalizing paths and ends in so many unexpected places.

Sometimes, the search itself is the most fulfilling: hearing a fascinating anecdote, uncovering an unknown piece of information, learning about a life-changing incident. Then researcher becomes writer, attempting to identify the subject's human essentials and enlarge the reader's understanding. Weaving collected tidbits together into a cohesive whole can give lifeblood to what was just a shadowy character on the page. I hope I have done that for Virginia Lee Burton; I hope I have increased your appreciation for her books, her art, and her extraordinary life.

REFERENCES ■

REFERENCES ■

GENERAL SOURCES

American Library Association Bulletin. June 1943.

Bader, Barbara. *American Picturebooks from Noah's Ark to the Beast Within.* New York: Macmillan, 1976.

Bohlin, Virginia. "Sculptor Lover of Life." *Gloucester Daily Times,* 10 September 1963.

Burns, Paul C., and Ruth Hines. "Virginia Lee Burton." *Elementary English,* April 1967.

Burton, Virginia Lee. Autobiographical brochure. Houghton Mifflin, n.d.

Burton, Virginia Lee. "Making Picture Books" Caldecott Medal speech in *Caldecott Medal Books: 1938–1957,* edited by Bertha Mahony Miller and Elinor Whitney Field. Boston: The Horn Book, 1957.

Burton, Virginia Lee. "Symphony in Comics." *The Horn Book,* July, 1941.

Colby, Jean Poindexter. "A Book Production Story." *The Horn Book,* March 1948.

Folly Cove Designers. Exhibition catalog. 7 May–31 October 1996. Gloucester: Cape Ann Historical Association.

Folly Cove Designers: A Retrospective. Exhibition catalog. 27 June–7 September 1982. Gloucester: Cape Ann Historical Association.

George Demetrios: Sculptor and Teacher: 1896–1974. Exhibition catalog. 1 August–15 November 1986. Gloucester: Cape Ann Historical Association.

Hogarth, Grace A. "Virginia Lee Burton, 1942 Caldecott Winner." *Library Journal,* 15 June 1943.

Howard, Robert West. "Designed in Folly Cove." *Country Gentleman,* February 1949.

Hoyle, Karen Nelson. "Virginia Lee Burton." In *Writers for Children,* compiled by Jane Bingham. New York: Scribners, 1988.

Kingman, Lee. "Virginia Lee Burton's Dynamic Sense of Design." Parts 1 and 2. *The Horn Book,* October and December 1970.

Kingman, Lee, et al. *Illustrators of Children's Books 1957–1966.* Boston: The Horn Book, 1968.

Lacy, Lyn. *Art and Design in Children's Picture Books: An Analysis of Caldecott Award–Winning Illustration.* Chicago: American Library Association, 1986.

Maletskos, Mary. "The Folly Cove World of Jinnee and George Demetrios." *Newsletter,* July–September, 1986. 6: 3. Gloucester: Cape Ann Historical Association.

Meigs, Cornelia, et al. *A Critical History of Children's Literature.* New York: Macmillan, 1953.

New England Craft Exhibition — 1955. Exhibition catalog. Worcester Art Museum, 12 October–27 November 1955. Worcester: Worcester Art Museum.

Schindel, Morton. Memo to Michael Demetrios. Kerlan Collection. University of Minnesota.

Schwartz, Joseph. *Ways of the Illustrator.* Chicago: American Library Association, 1982.

Stott, Jon C. "Virginia Lee Burton." In *American Writers for Children 1900–1960. Dictionary of Literary Biography* 22, Gale Research, 1983.

Thompson, Lovell. "The Versatility of Virginia Lee Burton." *Publishers Weekly,* 19 June 1943.

Viguers, Ruth Hill, et al. *Illustrators of Children's Books 1946–1956.* Boston: The Horn Book, 1958.

CHAPTER NOTES
Mary Anne Turns Sixty

1 The day of the groundbreaking: *Boston Sunday Globe,* November 14, 1999.

3 Burton described a book: Melanie L. Babendreier, "What Do You Do with a Steam Shovel Stuck in a Basement?" *Yankee,* December 1998.

Family Roots

7 Alfred Burton: *Who Was Who in America, 1897–1942.* Vol. 1. Chicago: Marquis Publishing, 1966.

Citations about his accomplishments: Henry E. Burroughs, *Boys in Men's Shoes: A World of Working Children.* New York: Macmillan, 1944.

8 Harold Burton: Letter, May 18, 1962. Cape Ann Historical Association.

Burton's mother: Bert Almon, "Jeanne D'Orge, Carmel, and Point Lobos." *Western American Literature,* fall 1994. Carl Cherry Foundation. Brochure, n.d.

Lena Dalkeith, *Aesop's Fables: Told to the Children,* with pictures by S. R. Praeger. New York: Dutton, circa 1908.

Lena Dalkeith, *Little Plays,* with pictures of little actors from photographs. London: T. C. & E. C. Jack, circa 1907.

Lena Dalkeith, *Stories from French History,* with pictures by Jenny Wylie. New York: Dutton, circa 1909.

10 his invention of the Cherry rivet: Robert Campbell, paper presented at the Sunset Center, Carmel, California, April 24, 2000.

Lena began using: The first known use of Jeanne D'Orge was on a poem published in the *Little Review* in 1916.

12 she won a scholarship: The California School of Fine Arts that Burton attended is now the College of the San Francisco Art Institute.

the high school yearbook: Virginia Lee Burton graduated from Sonora High School on June 13, 1927.

13 Muriel Stuart: Selma Jeanne Cohen, ed., *International Encyclopedia of Dance.* Vol. 5. New York: Oxford University Press, 1998.

Robert Hestwood: Peter Hastings Falk, ed., *Who Was Who in American Art: 1564–1975.* Madison, Conn.: Sound View Press, 1999.

14 She taught art: The Burroughs Newsboys Foundation was an organization established in 1927 to support working children; Burton's father served as educational director for a time.

known only as H.T.P.: Drama and music critic Henry Taylor Parker kept his identity a secret, causing much speculation in the Boston area arts community at the time. Biography Resource Center: Narrative Biographies. Detroit: Gale Group, 2000 (galenet.com).

Review of *Age of Innocence* in the *Boston Evening Transcript,* October 26, 1929.

15 "brilliant fluency": *George Demetrios: Sculptor and Teacher: 1896–1974.* Exhibition catalog. August 1–November 15, 1986. Gloucester: Cape Ann Historical Association.

From Jonnifer to Mike

24 "Sad-Faced Boy was a rush order": "The Hunt Breakfast." *Horn Book,* January/February 1939.

25 Her sons recall: "Dorgie" was the family name for George Demetrios; Burton used the nickname in her dedication of *The Little House.*
Shortly after publication: Ione Morrison Rider, "Arna Bontemps." *Horn Book,* January/February 1939.

26 "came from watching the engines": Comments appear on the back cover of the 1964 paperback of *Choo Choo.*
Mary Bacon Mason, *Fairies and Friendly Folk: Folk Song Pieces for the Piano.* Illus. by Virginia Demetrios. New York and Chicago: Clayton F. Summy, 1934. (Only published book known to bear her married name.)
L. Felix Ranlett, "Books and Two Small Boys." *Horn Book,* November 1942.
Robert McCloskey, *Lentil.* New York: Viking, 1940.
Ludwig Bemelmans, *Madeline.* New York: Viking, 1939.
Hardie Gramatky, *Little Toot.* New York: Putnam, 1939.
James Daugherty, *Andy and the Lion.* New York: Viking, 1938.

29 Her onetime editor: Interview with Mary Silva Cosgrave, one of Burton's former editors.
Review of *Choo Choo* in *Horn Book,* October 1937.

31 Review of Ethel Calvert Phillips's *Belinda and the Singing Clock* in *Booklist* 35 (November 1, 1938).

34 Hetty Burlington Beatty wrote and illustrated *The Little Wild Horse* (Houghton Mifflin, 1949); Milton Johnson illustrated Scott Odell's *Black Pearl* (Houghton Mifflin, 1967) and *The Dark Canoe* (Houghton Mifflin, 1968); and Fen Lasell illustrated *FlyAway Goose* (Houghton Mifflin, 1965). Ruth Hill Viguers, Marcia Dalphin, and Bertha Mahony Miller, eds., *Illustrators of Children's Books, 1946-1956.* Boston: Horn Book, 1958.

35 Tomie dePaola is the author-artist of many well-regarded children's books, including *Strega Nona* (Simon & Schuster, 1975) and *32 Fairmount Avenue* (Putnam, 1999).

A Golden Medal

46 Robert McCloskey, *Make Way for Ducklings.* New York: Viking, 1941.
H. A. Rey, *Curious George.* Boston: Houghton Mifflin, 1941.

Ruth Gannett, *My Father's Dragon.* New York: Random House, 1948.

51 *Parents* magazine found it: Quote comes from a Houghton Mifflin ad in *Library Journal,* June 15, 1943.

53 Nikolay Radlov, *The Cautious Carp and Other Fables in Pictures.* New York: Coward, McCann, 1938.
Helen Sewell, *Three Tall Tales.* New York: Macmillan, 1947.
Marcia Williams, *Greek Myths for Young Children.* Cambridge: Candlewick, 1995.
Avi, *City of Light, City of Darkness: A Comic Book Novel.* Illus. by Brian Floca. New York: Orchard, 1993.
Loreen Leedy, *The Furry News: How to Make a Newspaper.* New York: Holiday House, 1970.

57 Archival material reveals: Cape Ann Historical Association archives indicate that "The Little Pink House" was the working title for this book.

58 The work on *The Little House:* Letter to Lovell Thompson, May 14, 1957. Archives, Houghton Library, Harvard University.

64 Bill Peet: *Bill Peet: An Autobiography.* Boston: Houghton Mifflin, 1989.
Maurice Sendak, *Where the Wild Things Are.* New York: HarperCollins, 1963.
Chris Van Allsburg, *Jumanji.* Boston: Houghton Mifflin, 1981.

65 Anne Eaton, review of *The Little House* in *New York Times Book Review,* December 6, 1942.
Nicole Brodeur, "Children's Bedtime Story Is Sprawl Too Real for Us Grown-ups." *Seattle Times,* September 17, 2000.

66 Due to travel restrictions: "Newbery–Caldecott 1943 Awards." *Library Journal,* June 15, 1943.

67 Elizabeth Janet Gray, *Adam of the Road.* New York: Viking, 1942.
Mary and Conrad Buff, *Dash and Dart.* New York: Viking, 1942.
Clare Turlay Newberry, *Marshmallow.* New York: Harper, 1942.
The presentation fell on Flag Day: "John Newbery and

Randolph Caldecott Medals Awarded at Dinner for Librarians." *Publishers Weekly,* June 19, 1943.

Folly Cove Designers

69   heralded the show: "To Folly Cove Designers." *Gloucester Daily Times,* July 31, 1964.

76   ran full-page ads: Lord & Taylor full-page ads showcasing the five Folly Cove designs appeared in the *New York Times* and the *Boston Transcript,* August 26, 1945.
      Roger Babson, "A Lesson in Opportunity." *Washington Post,* September 17, 1945.
      requested that Babson's piece be read: *Congressional Record,* October 9, 1945, A4536.
      Folly Cove Designers: "Yankee Prints Get National Recognition." Photographs by Harold Carter. *Life* 19:22, November 26, 1945.

79   Furthermore, the demand for products: Narrative material, written by Pat Earle, to accompany the video of the Windhover Dancers presentation, *Once in Folly Cove.*

80   they donated all their sample books: An extensive collection of Folly Cove designs is located at the Cape Ann Historical Association.
      the beginnings of a book: Virginia Lee Burton, *Design and How!* (unpublished), Cape Ann Historical Association.
      adult trade book editor: Paul Brooks, undated memo, Cape Ann Historical Association.
      Over the next fifteen years: Letters concerning contract and letters about *Design and How!.* Archives, Houghton Library, Harvard University.

82   One group is trying to change that: The Windhover Dancers are directed by Ina Hahn, Burton's former dance teacher.

Katy, Robin, and Maybelle

86   Alvin Tresselt, *White Snow, Bright Snow.* Illus. by Roger Duvoisin. New York: Lothrop, 1947.

94   W. J. Stokoe, *The Observer's Book of British Wild Flowers.* London: Warne, n.d.
      William Rhind, *The History of the Vegetable Kingdom.* Glasgow: Blackie & Son, 1855.

The Waning Years

104   "The book is so grand": Bertha Mahony Miller, letter, May 13, 1962. Archives, Cape Ann Historical Association (Gloucester).

108   At the time of publication: Quote on dust jacket from Kirtley F. Mather, professor emeritus of geology, Harvard University.

109   translated into Japanese: *Gloucester Daily Times,* July 22, 1966.
      "like living in a Japanese print": Letter, March 24, 1964. Burton archives, Boston Public Library.

110   "No plot, no story": Sketchbook from archives, Cape Ann Historical Association.

111   Virginia Lee Burton died: October 15, 1968, at Peter Bent Brigham Hospital in Boston. Obituary notice, *New York Times,* October 16, 1968.

The Legend Lives On

113   Julia Sauer, *Mike's House.* New York: Viking, 1954.

114   Amy L. Cohn, "Bing! Bang! Crash! Slam! It's Mike Mulligan and Mary Anne!" *Horn Book Newsletter,* vol. 9, p. 1.
      Jim Trelease is the author of *The Read Aloud Handbook* (New York: Penguin Putnam, 1982).
      "How do you get to Popperville?": Burton archives, Boston Public Library.

116   Jay Leno, *Leading with My Chin.* New York: HarperCollins, 1996.

117   Norine Odland, "Books That Last." *Five Owls,* November/December 1987.
      Robert J. Samuelson, "Goodbye, Mike Mulligan." *Newsweek,* December 19, 1994.
      Robert Wright, "The Mike Mulligan Moment." *Time,* May 26, 1999.
      A. O. Scott, "The End of Innocence." *New York Times,* July 2, 2000.
      Jon Scieszka, *The Stinky Cheese Man.* Illus. by Lane Smith. New York: Viking, 1992.
      Janell Cannon, *Stellaluna.* San Diego: Harcourt, 1993.
      On the Web site: Five in a Row, book archives (www.five-inarow.com).

118 Phyllis Fenner, *The Proof of the Pudding.* New York: John Day, 1957.

"The Little House." *National Observer,* March 13, 1967.

119 Anne Tyler, "Why I Still Treasure *The Little House.*" *New York Times Book Review,* November 9, 1986.

120 Charles Clark, "Get 'Em While They're Young." *Historic Preservation,* July/August 1987.

Bill Peet, *Smokey.* Boston: Houghton Mifflin, 1962.

Hardie Gramatky, *Little Toot.* New York: Putnam, 1939.

William Pène du Bois, *The Flying Locomotive.* New York: Viking, 1941.

Wanda Gag, *Millions of Cats.* New York: Coward, McCann, 1928.

Boris Artzybasheff, *Seven Simeons.* New York: Viking, 1937.

James Mustich, *A Common Reader,* summer 2000. Pleasantville, New York: Akadine Press.

Archive Sources

Boston Public Library

Cape Ann Historical Association, Gloucester, Massachusetts

The Free Library of Philadelphia

Kerlan Collection at University of Minnesota

San Francisco Public Library

Sawyer Public Library, Gloucester, Massachusetts

University of Oregon

Interviews

Unless otherwise noted, information in this biography is from interviews with Burton's sons Aris and Michael Demetrios, her nephew Costa Maletskos, Dick Berkenbush, and Burton's former editor and close friend Lee Kingman Natti. Book data is from Houghton Mifflin.

Media Sources

The Little House. 8 min. Film. Burbank: Buena Vista Worldwide Services. Disney, o.p. 1951.

The Little House. Filmstrip. Narrated by Frances Kelley; music by Garry Sutliffe, Weston, Conn.: Weston Woods, 1972.

Mike Mulligan and His Steam Shovel. Narrated by Rod Ross; music by Arthur Kleiner. Filmstrip/cassette/paperback. Weston, Conn.: Weston Woods, 1989.

Mike Mulligan and His Steam Shovel. Videotape. Weston, Conn.: Weston Woods, 1956.

Mike Mulligan and His Steam Shovel. Produced by Michael Sporn. Videotape. New York: Ambrose Video, 1990.

Mike Mulligan and His Steam Shovel. CD-ROM. Boston: Houghton Mifflin, 1996.

Burton Bibliography (listed chronologically)

All titles, except those by Mason and Henderson, were published by Houghton Mifflin.

1934. Mason, Mary Bacon. *Fairies and Friendly Folk: Folk Song Pieces for the Piano.* Clayton F. Summy, o.p.

1937. Bontemps, Arna. *Sad-Faced Boy,* o.p.

1937. *Choo Choo: The Story of a Little Engine Who Ran Away.*

1938. Phillips, Ethel Calvert. *Belinda and the Singing Clock.* o.p.

1939. *Mike Mulligan and His Steam Shovel.*

1941. *Calico the Wonder Horse; or, The Saga of Stewy Slinker.* (Revised, 1951, with the title changed to *Calico the Wonder Horse; or, The Saga of Stewy Stinker*).

1941. Henderson, Kenneth A., editor. *Manual of American Mountaineering.* New York: Alpine Club.

1942. Henderson, Kenneth A., *Handbook of American Mountaineering.* Boston: Houghton Mifflin/Alpine Club. (Although not attributed, illustrations are probably by Virginia Lee Burton.)

1942. Bontemps, Arna, and Jack Conroy. *The Fast Sooner Hound.*

1942. Peck, Leigh. *Don Coyote.*

1942. *The Little House.*

1943. *Katy and the Big Snow.*

1947. Malcolmson, Anne, editor. *Song of Robin Hood.* Music by Grace Castagnetta.

1949. *The Emperor's New Clothes.*

1952. *Maybelle the Cable Car.*

1962. *Life Story: The Story of Life on Our Earth from Its Beginning Up to Now.*

ACKNOWLEDGMENTS

I WANT TO THANK THE MANY PEOPLE WHO WERE SO HELPFUL IN the preparation of this book. For taking time for questions and interviews and for generous lending of photographs and slides: Aris Demetrios, Michael Demetrios, Costa Maletskos, Dick and Sue Berkenbush, Mary Silva Cosgrave, and Lee Kingman Natti. For editorial direction and comments: Kim Keller, Anita Silvey, Carolyn Wiseman, Chere Elliott, and Karen Hanley. For input on specific questions and requests: Mary Beth Dunhouse, Jim Trelease, Roger Sutton, Gail Goss, Carolyn Field, Robert Campbell, Robert Reese of the Carl Cherry Foundation, and Tomie dePaola. Appreciation also goes to the curators and librarians in the various institutions that hold Burton materials. And thanks especially to Bear, for company, and to Don Elleman, who offered computer expertise, wisdom, support, and encouragement at every stage of this book's production.